ZERO TO ONE MILLION DOLLARS

By Cristian Tiru

Achieving Financial Prosperity: A Comprehensive Guide to Earning a Million Dollars in a Year

I0416142

Content:

Chapter 1: Laying the Groundwork -Cultivating a Mindset for Success

- Defining and Achieving Your Financial Ambitions

Chapter 2: Crafting a Robust Financial Blueprint

- Evaluating Your Present Financial Landscape
- Formulating a Feasible Financial Plan
- Establishing a Strategic Savings Framework

Chapter 3: Amplifying Earnings Potential

- Identifying High-Yeld Income Opportunities

- Transcending Limiting Beliefs and Overcoming Fears
- Nurturing Positivity and Building Resilience
- Embracing Failure as a Catalyst for Growth

Chapter 9: Architecting a Blueprint for Success

- Transcending Limiting Beliefs and Overcoming Fears
- Discovering High-Potential Business Ventures
- Amplifying Earnings Potential

Chapter 1: Laying the Groundwork

Cultivating a Mindset for Success

Embarking on the journey toward financial prosperity necessitates the development of an appropriate mindset. The foundation of any successful endeavor, especially one as ambitious as generating a million dollars in a single year from a standing start, lies in the mental preparedness and attitude of the individual. This section explores the critical role of mindset in driving financial achievement and outlines how adopting the correct psychological approach can significantly enhance your likelihood of reaching your monetary objectives.

Success, it must be understood, is seldom a product of mere fortune or happenstance. Rather, it emerges from a deliberate and conscious mindset—a mindset characterized by determination, resilience, and an unwavering commitment to achieving one's goals. Central to this mindset is the power of belief: a deep-seated conviction in one's capabilities and the determination to surmount any obstacle.

Vision is a pivotal element of a successful mindset.

Having a lucid and vivid picture of the life you aspire to and the financial targets you aim to hit is indispensable. This vision acts not only as a guide but also as a source of motivation and resilience during times of challenge, reminding you of the reasons behind your pursuit.

Resilience stands out as another cornerstone of the mindset required for success. The path to amassing a million dollars within a year is fraught with potential setbacks and hurdles. Those endowed with a resilient mindset, however, perceive these challenges as valuable learning opportunities and are adept at rebounding from setbacks, using them as catalysts for growth.

Equally important is the element of self-belief.

The conviction that earning a million dollars in a year is within your grasp can motivate you to embrace calculated risks, venture beyond your comfort zone, and capitalize on the opportunities that arise. This unwavering self-belief lays the groundwork for all subsequent achievements.

Moreover, a commitment to ongoing learning and self-enhancement is integral to a mindset geared toward success. Recognizing that knowledge and skills are ever-evolving, successful individuals are perpetual learners, constantly seeking new insights, abilities, and methodologies to stay at the forefront of their financial endeavors.

In essence, while specific strategies and actions are vital to generating a million dollars in a year, the underpinning mindset is what ultimately dictates success. Cultivating a mindset characterized by clarity of vision, resilience, self-belief, and an ongoing commitment to growth is paramount. With these mindset attributes firmly in place, navigating the complexities of financial achievement becomes a more structured and attainable endeavor.

Questionnaire: Cultivating a Mindset for Success

Section 1: Understanding the Importance of Mindset

Introduction to Mindset

- Do you believe that mindset plays a crucial role in achieving financial success? Why or why not?
- Can you describe a situation where your mindset significantly impacted your financial decisions?

Belief and Vision

- How strongly do you believe in your capability to achieve significant financial goals?
- Describe the vision you have for your financial future. How detailed is this vision?

Resilience and Challenges

- Reflect on a time when you faced a significant financial setback. How did you respond to it?
- On a scale of 1 to 10, how resilient do you consider yourself in the face of financial challenges?

Self-Belief and Risk-Taking

- How much do you agree with the statement: "I am confident in my ability to earn a million dollars in a year"?
- What is the biggest risk you have taken in pursuit of financial growth? Would you do it again?

Commitment to Learning

- How committed are you to ongoing learning and self-enhancement in the context of financial success?
- Can you list any books, courses, or seminars you have recently engaged with to improve your financial knowledge?

Section 2: Actionable Steps towards Cultivating a Successful Mindset

Developing a Clear Vision

- What steps can you take to clarify and enhance the vision for your financial future?
- How can you ensure that your vision remains a motivating factor for you?

Building Resilience

- Identify strategies you can adopt to strengthen your resilience against financial setbacks.
- How can you better prepare for potential financial challenges?

Enhancing Self-Belief

- What practical steps can you take to boost your self-belief in achieving your financial goals?
- How can you cultivate a more positive and empowering self-dialogue?

Committing to Continuous Learning

- List specific areas in finance or business where you feel you need more knowledge or skills.
- How do you plan to address these learning needs?

Applying the Mindset to Real-life Scenarios

- Given your current financial situation, what is one mindset shift you believe could make a significant difference?
- How will you implement this mindset shift in your daily life and financial decisions?

Reflection

- Reflecting on your answers, what are the key areas of mindset development you need to focus on?
- How do you plan to monitor and evaluate your progress in cultivating a mindset for success?
- This questionnaire is designed to provoke thought and encourage introspection on the fundamental aspects of cultivating a mindset for success in financial endeavors. By thoroughly engaging with these questions, you can identify areas for improvement and develop a strategic plan to enhance your financial success mindset.

Scoring Guide for the Questionnaire: Cultivating a Mindset for Success

The scoring guide below is designed to help you evaluate your responses to the questionnaire on cultivating a mindset for success. Each response will be scored on a scale from 1 to 5, where 1 indicates a low level of agreement or development in the mindset attribute, and 5 indicates a high level. The maximum possible score is 100, indicating a highly developed mindset for financial success.

Section 1: Understanding the Importance of Mindset

- Introduction to Mindset
- Recognition of mindset's role (1-5)
- Impact of mindset on financial decisions (1-5)
- Belief and Vision
- Strength of belief in capabilities (1-5)

- Clarity and detail of financial vision (1-5)
- Resilience and Challenges
- Response to financial setback (1-5)
- Self-rated resilience (1-5)
- Self-Belief and Risk-Taking
- Confidence in earning potential (1-5)
- Willingness to take financial risks (1-5)
- Commitment to Learning
- Commitment to financial learning (1-5)
- Engagement with learning resources (1-5)

Section 2: Actionable Steps towards Cultivating a Successful Mindset

- Developing a Clear Vision
- Steps to enhance financial vision (1-5)
- Motivation derived from vision (1-5)
- Building Resilience
- Strategies for resilience (1-5)
- Preparedness for financial challenges (1-5)
- Enhancing Self-Belief
- Steps to boost self-belief (1-5)
- Positive self-dialogue (1-5)
- Committing to Continuous Learning
- Identification of learning needs (1-5)
- Plan for addressing learning needs (1-5)
- Applying the Mindset to Real-life Scenarios
- Potential impact of mindset shift (1-5)
- Implementation of mindset shift (1-5)
- Reflection
- Key areas for mindset development (1-5)

- Plan for monitoring progress (1-5)

Total Score Calculation:

Add up the scores from each question to get your total score.

Maximum Score: 100

Interpretation of Scores:

- **80-100**: Highly developed mindset for financial success. You have a strong foundation and are well-prepared to pursue financial goals.
- **60-79:** Moderately developed mindset. You have a good understanding and some preparation but could benefit from focused improvement in certain areas.
- **40-59:** Developing mindset. You are in the early stages of cultivating a successful financial mindset and should focus on areas of weakness.
- **20-39:** Initial stages of mindset development. Considerable work is needed to build the foundational mindset for financial success.

1-19: Early understanding. Focus on learning and applying basic principles of a successful financial mindset.

This scoring guide is meant to provide insight into where you currently stand regarding the cultivation of a mindset for financial success and to help identify areas for growth and development.

Defining and Achieving Your Financial Ambitions

The initial step toward transforming the dream of millionaire status within a year into reality is the articulation of clear, achievable financial objectives. Regardless of your starting point—be it a nascent savings account or a blank financial slate—establishing a detailed plan is crucial for maintaining focus, motivation, and direction toward your financial summit. This subsection delves into the process of setting your financial goals and provides a framework for accruing one million dollars in a year from ground zero.

Commencing this journey requires introspection and clarity about your financial desires. Whether your aim is to eliminate debt, secure a down payment for a home, launch a business, or attain financial independence, understanding your personal aspirations is critical. This clarity will not only direct your financial path but also inspire and motivate you as you progress.

Upon identifying your financial ambitions, the next step involves breaking these goals down into tangible, manageable milestones. For instance, to save a million dollars within a year, delineate your targets into monthly, weekly, and daily savings benchmarks. This approach renders your overarching goal more approachable and facilitates the monitoring of your advancement.

Prioritizing your objectives based on their immediacy and significance is also essential. Assess which goals demand immediate action, like clearing high-interest debt, and which are more long-term endeavors, such as cultivating an investment portfolio. This prioritization enables the efficient allocation of resources and efforts.

Additionally, crafting a vision board or financial roadmap can be an influential motivator. This visual representation of your goals serves as a continuous reminder of your financial aspirations, aiding in the manifestation of your objectives and bolstering your resolve in the face of adversity.

In summary, the quest for millionaire status within a year is a discipline-intensive endeavor that demands a clear vision and strategic planning.

By defining your financial goals and breaking them down into actionable steps, you lay the foundation for a successful journey. Stay dedicated, be adaptable, and never underestimate your capacity to manifest financial prosperity.

Chapter 2: Crafting a Robust Financial Blueprint

Evaluating Your Present Financial Landscape

Prior to setting out on the ambitious endeavor to accumulate a million dollars within a single year, beginning from ground zero, it is imperative to conduct a thorough evaluation of your existing financial landscape. This foundational step is indispensable, as it lays the groundwork for your financial aspirations and equips you with the insights necessary to navigate your journey with informed precision. A meticulous understanding of your current financial status allows you to pinpoint potential constraints or opportunities that might influence your trajectory towards success.

Initiate this process by conducting an exhaustive analysis of your income streams against your expenditures. Calculate your total monthly earnings from all sources and juxtapose this figure with your monthly outgoings. Such an analysis is crucial for discerning whether you're operating at a surplus or a deficit each month. A clear grasp of your cash flow is essential, as it highlights areas for potential expenditure reduction or income augmentation.

Subsequently, conduct an assessment of your assets versus liabilities. Inventory your savings, investment portfolios, and any significant assets in your possession. Conversely, itemize your liabilities, including any outstanding debts, credit card balances, and mortgage obligations. This exercise sheds light on your net worth, delineating your financial health and any fiscal responsibilities requiring attention.

An evaluation of your current financial scenario also necessitates a review of your spending tendencies and financial objectives.

Scrutinize your expenditure patterns to unearth potential savings opportunities, thereby reallocating funds towards your ambitious goal of generating a million dollars within a year. Moreover, clearly articulate your short-term and long-term financial aspirations, providing a quantifiable target to guide your fiscal endeavors.

Moreover, an appraisal of your risk tolerance and financial acumen is essential. Gauge your comfort level with risk and ascertain whether your financial literacy is sufficient for making informed investment decisions. If necessary, embark on a journey of financial education or seek professional advice to enhance your success potential.

In summary, a comprehensive evaluation of your current financial status forms the cornerstone of your endeavor to amass a million dollars within a year. By gaining insight into your income, expenses, assets, liabilities, and by understanding your spending habits, financial goals, risk tolerance, and knowledge, you are better positioned to make strategic decisions and implement actionable steps towards realizing your financial aspirations. This evaluation not only serves as the bedrock of your financial journey but also as a strategic compass guiding you towards future success.

Formulating a Feasible Financial Plan

Embarking on the path to financial achievement, particularly with the ambitious goal of amassing a million dollars within a year, necessitates the formulation of a feasible and detailed financial plan. This chapter is dedicated to guiding you through the critical steps required to develop a budget that not only aligns with but also facilitates the realization of your financial dreams, whether starting anew or building upon an existing foundation.

Initially, it is crucial to gain a comprehensive understanding of your financial standing. Catalogue all sources of income, expenses, debts, and other financial commitments to paint a detailed picture of your fiscal condition. This step is pivotal in determining the extent of savings or investments needed to reach your seven-figure target.

Upon clarifying your financial situation, the next phase involves establishing realistic financial objectives. Ascertain the amount needed to be saved or earned each month to meet your goal, breaking it down into smaller, more manageable milestones to mitigate feelings of overwhelm.

A critical component of this plan is the meticulous tracking of your expenditures. Pinpoint areas where expenditure can be minimized, thereby prioritizing your financial objectives and ensuring the optimal allocation of funds. Remember, each dollar saved is a stride closer to your million-dollar mark.

With a clear understanding of your financial goals and expenditures, proceed to create your budget. Segregate your expenses into fixed and variable categories. Fixed expenses encompass rent, utilities, and loan repayments, whereas variable expenses cover groceries, entertainment, and other discretionary spends.

Allocate a specific sum to each category, ensuring alignment with your financial objectives. Factor in unforeseen expenses by establishing a contingency fund to mitigate potential financial disruptions.

The efficacy of your budget hinges on regular monitoring and adjustments as needed. Conduct monthly reviews of your budget, making amendments to address any consistent overspending in particular categories.

Constructing a realistic budget is a fundamental stride towards achieving your million-dollar ambition. By thoroughly understanding your financial landscape, setting attainable goals, diligently tracking expenses, and consistently reviewing your budget, you lay a solid foundation for financial success.

Persistence and discipline are key; with a meticulously planned budget, the realization of your financial aspirations is within reach.

Establishing a Strategic Savings Framework

The quest for financial prosperity, underscored by the goal of evolving from zero to millionaire status within a year, underscores the criticality of instituting a strategic savings framework. Independent of one's current financial bearings, the adoption of a savings strategy is a pragmatic step instrumental in facilitating the accumulation of a million dollars within the stipulated timeframe.

The inception of a savings strategy is predicated on budget formulation. Undertake a holistic review of your income juxtaposed against your expenditures. Identify avenues for expenditure reduction, thereby augmenting your savings potential. This endeavor might necessitate lifestyle adjustments and sacrifices; however, it's paramount to remember that each increment saved edifies your financial objectives.

Subsequent to budget creation, delineate a savings objective. Specify a monthly savings target and earmark a designated portion of your income towards achieving this goal. Adhere steadfastly to this savings target, and contemplate the automation of savings through scheduled transfers to a dedicated savings account, circumventing the temptation to divert these funds elsewhere.

An integral component of your savings strategy is the eradication of non-essential debt. The presence of high-interest debt, such as credit card obligations and loans, can significantly impede your journey towards the million-dollar milestone. Devise a systematic debt repayment strategy, prioritizing debts with the highest interest rates. As debts are retired, reallocate the funds previously dedicated to debt servicing towards bolstering your savings.

Beyond traditional savings vehicles, explore diversified savings and investment options. Investigate high-yield savings accounts, certificates of deposit, and equity markets.

Diversification not only enhances the growth potential of your savings but also optimizes the efficiency of your capital accumulation efforts.

Lastly, it's imperative to periodically assess your savings strategy's effectiveness. Regularly revisit and refine your approach to ensure alignment with your financial objectives. Acknowledge and celebrate milestones as they occur, maintaining motivation by envisaging the ultimate reward of achieving a million dollars within a year.

In essence, the development of a savings strategy demands discipline and unwavering commitment. Although the path may present challenges, the long-term rewards of financial autonomy and prosperity overwhelmingly justify the short-term sacrifices.

By implementing these strategic steps and remaining dedicated to your savings objectives, the transformation of your financial status from zero to millionaire becomes not just plausible, but achievable.

Questionnaire: Defining and Achieving Your Financial Ambitions

Section 1: Goal Setting and Financial Vision

- Have you clearly articulated your financial goals for the next year?
- Do you have a specific financial objective, such as earning a million dollars within a year?
- How detailed is your plan for reaching your financial ambitions?

Section 2: Evaluating Your Financial Landscape

- Have you conducted a thorough evaluation of your current financial situation?
- Do you regularly analyze your income versus expenditures to identify potential savings?
- Have you assessed your assets and liabilities to understand your net worth?

Section 3: Crafting a Financial Plan

- Have you established realistic financial objectives based on your current financial situation?
- Are you tracking your expenditures to identify areas where you can save more?
- Have you created a budget that aligns with your financial goals?

Section 4: Establishing a Savings Strategy

- Do you have a clear savings target each month to help you reach your financial goal?
- Have you considered automating your savings to ensure consistency?
- Are you actively working on reducing non-essential debt to free up more funds for savings?
- Have you explored diversified savings and investment options to maximize your savings growth?

Scoring

Each question can be scored as follows, with the total providing an insight into your readiness and strategy for achieving your financial ambitions:

- Yes, definitely (5 points): You're actively engaged in this aspect of your financial planning.
- Somewhat (3 points): You've made some progress but have more to do in this area.
- Not really (1 point): This is an area you need to work on significantly.
- No, not at all (0 points): You have not addressed this aspect of your financial planning.

Total Score Calculation

- **52-65 points:** You're well on your way to defining and achieving your financial ambitions with a solid plan in place.
- **39-51 points:** You've made a good start but need to refine your strategies and implementation.
- **26-38 points:** There's work to be done in clarifying your goals, evaluating your financial landscape, and crafting a detailed financial plan.
- **0-25 points:** It's time to start taking your financial ambitions seriously by setting clear goals, evaluating your finances, and developing a comprehensive plan.

This scoring system helps identify areas of strength in your financial planning and areas that require more attention to ensure you're on the path to achieving your financial ambitions.

Cultivating a Success Mindset

2.Vision and Goal Setting

3.Resilience in the Face of Challenges

4.Self-Belief and Confidence

5.Continuos Learning and Growth

6.Defining Financial Ambitions

7.Breaking Down Goals into Achievable Steps

8.Creating a Vision Board

To effectively navigate and apply the insights from the text I have shared with you , please find herebelow a suggestion of a step-by-step guide designed to you to absorb and implement the knowledge presented:

Step 1: Self-Assessment and Mindset Adjustment

- Reflect on your current mindset regarding wealth and success. Recognize any limiting beliefs and commit to adopting a growth and success-oriented mindset.
- Complete the questionnaire provided in the text to assess your current mindset and readiness for financial success. This will help identify areas for improvement.

Step 2: Goal Setting and Visualization

- Define clear, specific financial goals for the short term (1 year) and long term (5 years and beyond). Make them SMART: Specific, Measurable, Achievable, Relevant, and Time-bound.
- Create a vision board or write a detailed description of your life once you achieve these financial goals. Regularly visualize your success to maintain motivation.

Step 3: Financial Analysis and Planning

- Conduct a thorough review of your current financial situation, including income, expenses, assets, and liabilities.

- Identify areas for cost reduction and increase in income. This might involve budget adjustments, lifestyle changes, and exploring additional income streams.
- Develop a detailed financial plan that outlines steps to achieve your goals, including savings targets, investment strategies, and debt reduction plans.

Step 4: Implementation and Discipline

- Implement your financial plan with discipline. Use tools like budget trackers, financial planning apps, or spreadsheets to monitor your progress.
- Adjust your plan as necessary, based on changes in your financial situation or goals.

Step 5: Education and Growth

- Commit to continuous learning about personal finance, investment, and wealth management. Read books, attend workshops, or take courses to enhance your knowledge and skills.
- Network with successful individuals who have achieved similar financial goals. Learn from their experiences and apply relevant advice to your situation.

Step 6: Resilience and Persistence

- Prepare for setbacks and challenges. Develop resilience by viewing failures as learning opportunities.

- Stay persistent in your efforts. Remember that achieving significant financial success often takes time and continuous effort.

Step 7: Evaluation and Adjustment

- Regularly evaluate your financial progress against your goals. Use the scoring guide provided in the text to assess your mindset and strategy effectiveness.
- Make necessary adjustments to your financial plan and strategies based on your evaluation.

Step 8: Reflection and Mindset Reinforcement

- Reflect on your journey periodically. Acknowledge your achievements and areas of improvement.
- Reinforce a positive and success-oriented mindset. Celebrate successes, no matter how small, to maintain motivation and commitment to your financial goals.

Step 9: Sharing and Mentoring

- Once you've made significant progress or achieved your goals, consider sharing your knowledge and experiences with others. Mentoring or guiding others can reinforce your own understanding and commitment to financial success.

Step 10: Scaling and Diversification

- Explore opportunities for scaling your income and diversifying your investment portfolio. Consider more advanced financial strategies to protect and grow your wealth further.

Chapter 3.Amplifying Earnings Potential

Identifying High-Yield Income Opportunities

In the contemporary era, the quest for financial prosperity and the ambition to amass a fortune within a mere year are aspirations harbored by many. Nevertheless, the journey to accrue a million dollars within such a tight timeframe can appear formidable, if not insurmountable, to the majority. This section, titled "Identifying High-Yield Income Opportunities," is designed to outline actionable strategies that can transform these lofty dreams into tangible outcomes, irrespective of one's financial starting point.

Before exploring the myriad of income-generating avenues, it's paramount to recognize that achieving such an ambitious financial milestone necessitates unwavering commitment, resilience, and an adventurous spirit to venture beyond familiar territories. The methodologies recommended herein are not mere shortcuts to wealth but rather time-tested approaches that have propelled numerous individuals towards substantial financial prosperity.

Entrepreneurship stands out as a premier avenue for wealth creation. Embarking on an entrepreneurial venture offers the dual benefits of generating multiple income streams and exercising autonomy over one's financial future.

This guide delves into critical aspects of entrepreneurship such as pinpointing lucrative market niches, crafting a comprehensive business strategy, securing capital, and deploying effective marketing tactics to guarantee success.

Investment is another critical pillar explored in depth. Despite its perceived complexity, this guide demystifies the investment landscape, spotlighting a variety of investment vehicles including equities, real estate, and digital currencies. It equips readers with essential knowledge to make astute investment choices and optimize the growth of their capital.

Moreover, this section underscores the significance of harnessing digital advancements and the online ecosystem. The digital revolution has unlocked a plethora of opportunities to generate income through avenues such as affiliate marketing, e-commerce, freelance work, and digital product creation. This guide provides a comprehensive roadmap for navigating these digital income streams.

Additionally, the guide emphasizes the importance of mastering high-demand skills.

By acquiring expertise in sought-after domains like software development, digital marketing, or design, individuals can distinguish themselves as highly valued professionals, thereby unlocking avenues for premium compensation.

In essence, "Identifying High-Yield Income Opportunities" offers a navigational blueprint for individuals eager to embark on the journey towards amassing a million dollars within a year. Through a blend of practical advice, insightful strategies, and real-world examples, this guide empowers individuals from diverse backgrounds to seize control of their financial destiny and realize their millionaire aspirations. Whether one is a recent graduate, a homemaker, or an experienced professional yearning for change, this section offers valuable insights for anyone poised to transform their financial dreams into reality.

Harnessing Personal Skills and Talents for Financial Gain

Recognizing and leveraging one's innate skills and talents is fundamental in charting a course towards significant financial achievement. Irrespective of one's background or present circumstances, this subsection is dedicated to guiding individuals through the process of utilizing their inherent abilities to achieve the monumental goal of generating a million dollars within a year, starting from scratch.

The initial step involves an introspective analysis to identify one's core strengths and unique talents. Whether your forte lies in creative writing, persuasive communication, or analytical problem-solving, acknowledging these competencies is the first stride towards financial success. By pinpointing areas of natural proficiency, you can concentrate your endeavors where you have a competitive edge, thereby enhancing your likelihood of success. Subsequently, it's imperative to refine these skills. Dedicate time and resources to polish your abilities, whether through formal education, self-directed online learning, or practical application. Advancing your skillset not only bolsters your self-confidence but also amplifies your market value, paving the way for lucrative opportunities.

Identifying potential niches that align with your skillset is another critical step. Conduct market research to uncover sectors where your talents are in high demand. By catering to niche markets, you can establish yourself as a distinguished expert, commanding higher fees for your services or products. Networking also plays a crucial role in the monetization of your skills and talents. Forge connections with peers, industry leaders, and prospective clients. Participate in professional gatherings, join relevant associations, and engage in digital forums to broaden your professional network.

Collaborations and insights gleaned from your network can unlock new avenues for income generation. Perseverance and a commitment to lifelong learning are indispensable in this endeavor. Amassing wealth swiftly necessitates dedication, the capacity to rebound from setbacks, and an unwavering commitment to personal and professional growth. View challenges as opportunities for learning, adapt to evolving market needs, and steadfastly pursue your financial objectives.

In sum, harnessing your personal skills and talents is a pivotal strategy in the journey to earning a million dollars within a year from scratch. By identifying and developing your unique abilities, targeting specific niches, expanding your professional network, and embracing continuous improvement, you can unlock your full potential and embark on a remarkable path to financial abundance. Emboldened by your unique capabilities, take decisive action and watch as your skills pave the way to achieving your millionaire dreams in record time.

Questionnaire: Amplifying Earnings Potential and Identifying High-Yield Income Opportunities

Section 1: Entrepreneurship and Business Ventures

- Have you considered starting your own business or entrepreneurial venture as a way to increase your income?
- Do you have a specific market niche or business idea you believe has high earning potential?
- How knowledgeable are you about securing capital and deploying effective marketing strategies for a business?

Section 2: Investments

- Are you familiar with different investment vehicles like equities, real estate, and digital currencies?
- How confident are you in making investment choices that could optimize the growth of your capital?

Section 3: Digital Opportunities

- Have you explored earning income through digital avenues such as affiliate marketing, e-commerce, or freelance work?

- How comfortable are you with utilizing digital platforms to generate income?

Section 4: Skill Development and Monetization

- Have you conducted an introspective analysis to identify your core strengths and unique talents?
- Are you actively refining your skills through education, online learning, or practical application?
- Have you identified potential niches where your skills are in high demand?
- How engaged are you in networking to monetize your skills and talents?

Scoring

Rate each question based on the following scale to assess your readiness and potential strategies for amplifying your earnings potential:

- Strongly Agree (5 points): You're actively engaged and have a strong foundation in this area.
- Agree (4 points): You have some experience or knowledge, with room for improvement.
- Neutral (3 points): You're aware but haven't taken significant steps in this direction.
- Disagree (2 points): You have limited experience or knowledge.
- Strongly Disagree (1 point): You have not considered or engaged in this area at all.

Total Score Calculation

- **44-55 points:** You are well-prepared to amplify your earnings potential, with strong foundations across key areas.
- **33-43 points:** You have a moderate understanding and some preparation but need to focus on developing certain areas further.
- **22-32 points:** Your readiness is developing; focusing on specific areas could significantly enhance your earning potential.
- **11-21 points:** There's substantial room for growth in understanding and leveraging high-yield income opportunities.

Reflection

Based on your total score, consider which areas require more focus to maximize your earnings potential. Reflect on steps you can take to enhance your knowledge, skills, and strategies in those areas. Remember, achieving significant financial growth is a continuous learning process that requires dedication, resilience, and an adventurous spirit.

Cultivating Diverse Revenue Streams

In the dynamically evolving economic landscape of today, reliance on a singular income source is insufficient for attaining financial independence. The aspiration to generate a million dollars in a year from ground zero necessitates the exploration and development of multiple income streams. This subsection is dedicated to equipping individuals, regardless of their prior knowledge or experience, with the strategies required to establish and nurture these diverse revenue channels, thereby facilitating their journey towards millionaire status.

The inception of multiple income streams begins with the diversification of one's skillset. Identify your inherent strengths, passions, and interests, and explore avenues to monetize these attributes. Whether it involves freelancing, consulting, or initiating a side venture, utilizing your skills beyond conventional employment can yield additional income sources. The broader and more varied your skillset, the greater your opportunities for income generation.

Investing in assets that produce income is another pivotal strategy. This can encompass a spectrum from real estate to equities, bonds, or starting an investment portfolio. By judiciously allocating your resources into these assets, you can cultivate passive income streams that contribute to your overall wealth. It is, however, essential to engage in comprehensive research and possibly consult with financial experts to navigate these investment choices wisely.

Moreover, capitalizing on the digital revolution is imperative. Consider launching an online enterprise, such as an e-commerce platform, affiliate marketing, or digital product creation. The global reach of the internet offers an unparalleled opportunity to attract a vast customer base and generate revenue around the clock. Establishing a strong online presence through social media and a professionally crafted website is crucial for maximizing the potential of your online income sources.

Passive income avenues, including royalties from intellectual property like books, music, or patents, should not be overlooked. Creating valuable content or innovations and leveraging them across multiple platforms can result in ongoing income without the need for active involvement.

Networking and strategic collaborations are also key elements in the creation of multiple income streams.

Surround yourself with individuals who share your aspirations, participate in industry conferences, engage in mastermind groups, and seek mentorship from those who have attained financial success. Collaborating with others can unveil new opportunities and facilitate access to diverse income channels.

In conclusion, the development of multiple income streams is a critical facet of the strategy to amass a million dollars within a year from scratch. Through skill diversification, investment in income-generating assets, leveraging digital platforms, exploring passive income opportunities, and engaging in networking, you can significantly enhance your income potential and expedite your journey to financial freedom. Remember, achieving remarkable financial outcomes demands determination, adaptability, and a proactive approach to stepping out of your comfort zone.

Chapter 4: Strategic Investment for Growth and Wealth Accumulation

Foundational Investment Concepts

Investment strategies are pivotal in navigating the path towards financial prosperity and the accumulation of wealth.

This subchapter delves into the core principles of investment strategies, elucidating how they can facilitate the ambitious goal of earning a million dollars within a mere year, starting from zero. Catering to both seasoned investors and novices, grasping these foundational concepts is crucial for anyone intent on realizing their financial aspirations.

Investing embodies the principle of employing your capital in a manner that it generates returns, serving as a proactive alternative to merely hoarding your funds. It entails the judicious distribution of resources across various assets with the aim of reaping benefits over time. However, it's important to recognize that investing is not a monolithic approach; it encompasses a variety of strategies, each tailored to specific objectives, risk tolerances, and temporal frameworks.

A principal strategy that will be explored is the concept of diversification. This strategy advocates for the allocation of investments across a diverse range of assets including stocks, bonds, real estate, and commodities, thereby mitigating the risks associated with any single investment and enhancing the probability of achieving consistent returns.

Asset allocation, another critical strategy, involves determining the ideal composition of assets within your portfolio, aligned with your risk appetite and goals. For instance, a younger investor with a penchant for risk might allocate a larger portion of their portfolio to stocks, known for their potential for high returns albeit accompanied by increased volatility. Conversely, a more risk-averse investor might prefer a greater emphasis on bonds, which offer stability and regular income.

The strategy of long-term investing will also be highlighted. This approach emphasizes the importance of maintaining a broad perspective, undeterred by short-term market fluctuations. Adopting a long-term investment strategy allows for the benefit of compounding returns and the ability to weather market downturns, ultimately maximizing wealth accumulation.

Moreover, the necessity of informed decision-making in investments is underscored. This includes a thorough understanding of the assets under consideration, an analysis of market trends, and staying abreast of economic developments that could influence your investment outcomes.

In summary, mastering investment strategies is an indispensable component of the journey from zero to millionaire. Through diversification, strategic asset allocation, a commitment to long-term investing, and informed decision-making, you enhance your prospects of achieving your financial goals. Remember, successful investing is an ongoing educational journey, and with the appropriate strategies in play, your aspirations of financial success are well within reach.

Navigating the Investment Landscape for Maximum Returns

To achieve the monumental goal of generating a million dollars within a year from a standing start, it's imperative to grasp the significance of meticulously researching and selecting profitable investments.

This subsection is crafted to provide actionable insights that will steer individuals towards informed investment decisions, propelling them towards their financial objectives.

Embarking on this investment journey necessitates a foundational education on the array of investment options available. This encompasses a deep dive into various asset classes including equities, bonds, real estate, and mutual funds.

By cultivating an understanding of the distinct characteristics and inherent risks of each asset class, investors are better positioned to make savvy investment choices.

Conducting exhaustive research on potential investment opportunities is the next critical step. This involves a rigorous analysis of financial performance indicators, market trends, and the future outlook of potential investments. Utilizing financial news outlets, analytical reports, and digital platforms that offer in-depth insights into stocks, corporations, and industry dynamics is a highly effective strategy for this purpose.

The principle of diversification is paramount in the selection of profitable investments. By allocating your investments across a varied spectrum of asset classes and sectors, you can diminish the overall risk profile of your portfolio. In the event that one investment underperforms, the diversified nature of your portfolio can help counterbalance any potential losses. Achieving diversification can be realized through a mix of stocks, bonds, real estate investments, among others.

Time horizon alignment with investment goals is also essential. Investments tailored for short-term objectives might necessitate a more conservative approach, whereas long-term ambitions can accommodate a higher degree of risk for the sake of greater potential returns. Ensuring that your investment strategy is congruent with your financial aims is key to success.

The counsel of financial professionals can provide invaluable insights when navigating investment selections.

Financial advisors offer expert advice, tailored to your unique needs and risk tolerance, assisting in the identification of profitable investment opportunities and the formulation of a balanced investment portfolio.

Ongoing monitoring and evaluation of your investments are indispensable. As market conditions evolve, staying informed and ready to adjust your investment strategy accordingly is crucial. Regular assessment of your portfolio's performance and strategic realignment with your investment objectives ensures you remain on the path to achieving your goal of a million dollars within a year.

In conclusion, the process of researching and selecting profitable investments is a vital component of the strategy to amass a million dollars within a year from scratch.

Through dedicated self-education, thorough investment research, embracing diversification, aligning investments with financial goals, seeking expert advice, and vigilant portfolio management, you elevate your chances of attaining financial success. Patience, discipline, and a perspective geared towards the long term are indispensable virtues in the wealth-building journey through strategic investments.

Questionnaire: Strategic Investment for Growth and Wealth Accumulation

Foundational Investment Concepts

- Understanding Investment Basics
- Do you understand the basic principles of investing, including the need for generating returns on capital?
- How familiar are you with the concept of diversification in investment?

Strategic Asset Allocation

- Have you determined your risk appetite and aligned it with your investment portfolio composition?
- Do you have a strategy for allocating assets in your portfolio based on your long-term financial goals?

Approach to Long-term Investing

- How committed are you to maintaining a long-term perspective in your investment decisions?
- Are you prepared to navigate through short-term market fluctuations without compromising your investment strategy?

Informed Decision-Making

- How often do you conduct thorough research before making investment decisions?
- Do you stay updated on market trends and economic developments that could affect your investments?
- Navigating the Investment Landscape for Maximum Returns

Researching Investment Options

- Are you actively educating yourself on various asset classes and their characteristics?
- How rigorous is your approach to analyzing financial performance indicators and market trends for potential investments?

Diversification for Profitable Investments

- Do you implement diversification across different asset classes and sectors in your investment portfolio?
- How do you balance the risk and return in your investment choices to achieve optimal portfolio diversification?

Aligning Time Horizon with Investment Goals

- Is your investment strategy tailored to match your short-term and long-term financial objectives?
- How frequently do you review and adjust your investment plan to ensure alignment with your financial goals?

Seeking Professional Advice

- Have you considered consulting with a financial advisor to enhance your investment strategy?
- How valuable do you find professional financial advice in making investment decisions?

Portfolio Monitoring and Adjustment

- Do you regularly monitor your investment portfolio's performance?
- How proactive are you in adjusting your investment strategy based on market conditions and performance analysis?

Scoring

- **Strongly Agree (5 points):** Indicates high engagement and proactive behavior in investment strategies.
- **Agree (4 points):** Shows a good level of involvement and understanding with room for further development.
- **Neutral (3 points):** Reflects an average level of engagement, indicating potential areas for growth.
- **Disagree (2 points):** Suggests limited involvement or understanding, highlighting areas for improvement.
- **Strongly Disagree (1 point):** Demonstrates a lack of engagement or understanding in key investment areas.

Total Score Calculation

Sum of all responses: The total score will indicate your overall readiness and strategic positioning for investment growth and wealth accumulation.

Interpretation

- **41-45 points:** Excellent understanding and application of strategic investment principles for wealth accumulation.
- **31-40 points:** Good foundation in investment strategies with some areas to enhance for better growth.
- **21-30 points:** Moderate understanding; significant room for improvement in strategic investment practices.
- **11-20 points:** Limited grasp of investment concepts; essential to focus on educational and practical investment aspects.
- **9-10 points:** Minimal engagement with investment strategies; critical need for foundational investment education and practice.

This scoring system is designed to help you assess your preparedness and strategic approach towards investing for growth and wealth accumulation. Identifying areas of strength and those requiring improvement can guide your efforts to enhance your investment knowledge and practices.

1Financial Landscape Overview.

2.Income VS Expenses Comparison

3.Asset and Liability Inventory

4.Spending Habits Analysis

5. Setting Financial Goals

6.Creating a Realistic Budget

7.Expense Tracking and Reduction

8.Saving Goal Jar

9.Debt Elimination Strategy

10.Saving and Investment Growth

Chapter 5: Elevating Investment Portfolio Diversification

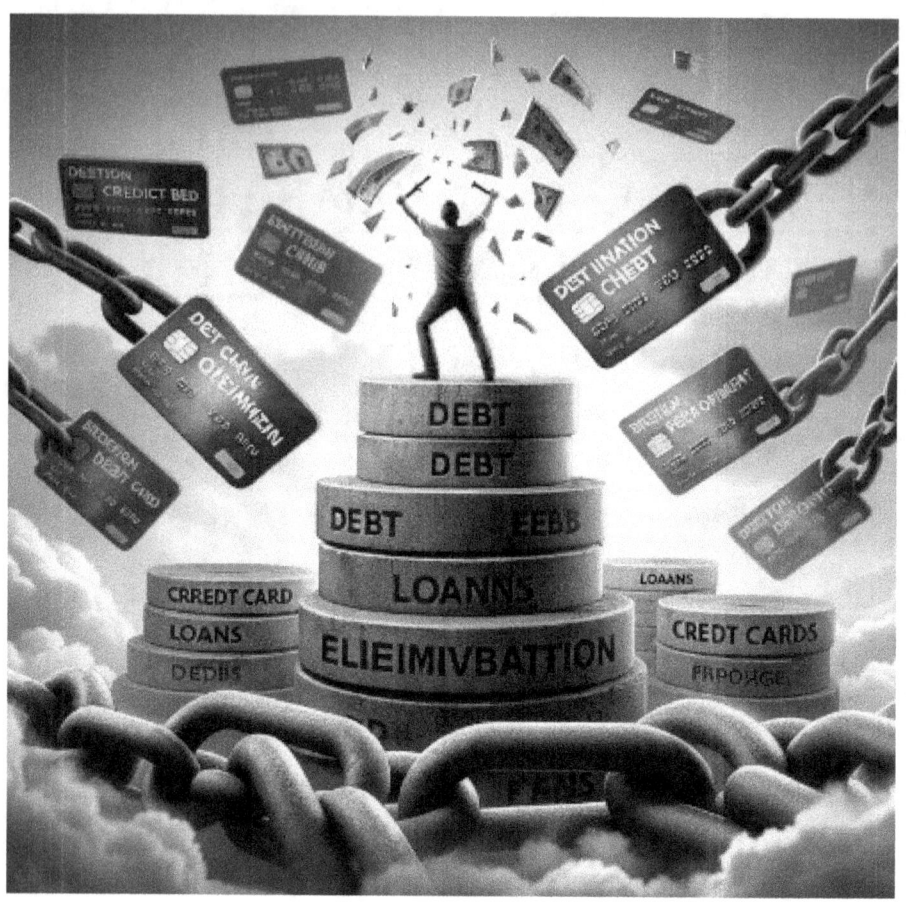

Strategic Diversification for Wealth Accumulation

In the realm of wealth creation and financial prosperity, diversifying your investment portfolio stands out as a pivotal strategy often underestimated by many.

This section delves into the critical importance of diversification and outlines actionable measures to enhance your investment returns, thereby elevating your likelihood of amassing a million dollars within a year from the ground up.

Diversification serves as a cornerstone for mitigating risk while simultaneously amplifying potential returns. By allocating your investments across various asset classes, sectors, and geographic territories, you can significantly dampen the adverse effects of any single investment's underperformance on your portfolio's overall health. This strategic spread ensures that potential downturns in one area may be counterbalanced by gains in another, maintaining a stable growth trajectory.

Initiating portfolio diversification entails identifying a spectrum of asset classes that resonate with your financial objectives and risk appetite. A well-rounded portfolio might include equities, bonds, real estate, mutual funds, exchange-traded funds (ETFs), and even alternative investments like digital currencies or commodities. Each asset class bears its own set of risks and rewards, necessitating a thorough evaluation and understanding before investment.

Further diversification within each asset class is also essential. For stocks, this means investing across a wide array of sectors such as technology, healthcare, finance, and energy. In real estate, consider spreading investments across different geographical locations or property types (residential, commercial, industrial).

Expanding your investment horizon to include international markets can also introduce new growth opportunities and additional diversification benefits. Emerging markets, in particular, may offer substantial growth potential but come with higher risk levels that require careful consideration.

Regular portfolio review and rebalancing are vital to maintaining optimal diversification. Market dynamics can shift the balance of your investments over time, necessitating adjustments to realign with your original diversification strategy and financial goals.

In summary, achieving a diversified investment portfolio is a deliberate step towards the ambitious goal of earning a million dollars within a year. Through careful selection and allocation across diverse asset classes, sectors, and regions, you can minimize risks and position yourself for sustained financial growth.

It is essential to conduct comprehensive research, continually assess your investment landscape, and adjust your strategy to navigate towards long-term financial success and reach your million-dollar milestone.

To effectively utilize the knowledge from the chapters on amplifying earnings potential, strategic investment, and diversification for wealth accumulation, I would suggest to follow these practical steps. This guide is trying to translate the concepts and strategies into actionable tasks that can help achieve the ambitious goal of generating significant financial growth within a year.

Amplifying Earnings Potential

Entrepreneurship Exploration:

- Brainstorm business ideas based on your interests, market needs, and potential for high returns.
- Conduct market research to validate your idea and identify your target audience.
- Develop a business plan outlining your strategy, financial projections, and marketing approach.

Investment in Skills:

- Identify skills in high demand within your industry or areas you're passionate about.
- Invest in courses, certifications, or workshops to enhance your expertise.

Digital Income Streams:

- Explore online platforms for freelancing, affiliate marketing, or creating and selling digital products.
- Build a personal brand on social media to attract opportunities and establish credibility.

Networking:

- Attend industry events, seminars, and workshops to connect with like-minded professionals.
- Join online forums and social media groups related to your field to exchange knowledge and find collaborations.
- Strategic Investment for Growth and Wealth Accumulation

Education on Investment:

- Dedicate time to learn about various investment vehicles (stocks, bonds, real estate, etc.).
- Use online resources, books, and courses to build your investment knowledge.

Market Research:

- Regularly follow financial news, market trends, and investment analyses.
- Utilize financial tools and platforms for in-depth research on potential investments.

Diversification Strategy:

- Allocate investments across different asset classes to spread risk.
- Consider long-term and short-term investments based on your financial goals.

Professional Advice:

- If possible, consult with a financial advisor to tailor your investment strategy to your personal risk tolerance and goals.
- Use robo-advisors for automated, algorithm-based investment recommendations.

Portfolio Review:

- Regularly assess your investment portfolio's performance.
- Rebalance your portfolio as needed to maintain alignment with your diversification strategy and financial objectives.
- Elevating Investment Portfolio Diversification

Asset Class Exploration:

- Research and identify various asset classes that align with your risk tolerance and financial goals.
- Diversify investments within each asset class (e.g., different sectors, industries, and geographies).

International Investments:

- Explore opportunities in emerging markets and international funds to add to your portfolio.
- Be aware of the risks and perform due diligence before investing in foreign markets.

Alternative Investments:

- Consider adding alternative investments like real estate, commodities, or digital currencies to your portfolio for further diversification.
- Understand the unique risks and opportunities each alternative investment presents.

Continuous Learning:

- Stay informed about global economic trends, market conditions, and new investment opportunities.
- Attend webinars, subscribe to investment newsletters, and follow thought leaders in the investment community.

Rebalancing Schedule:

- Set a regular schedule (e.g., quarterly, semi-annually) to review and rebalance your portfolio.
- Adjust your investment strategy based on performance, life changes, or shifts in financial goals.

Chapter 6: Capitalizing on Entrepreneurial Ventures

Discovering High-Potential Business Ventures

Attaining the lofty goal of generating a million dollars within a year necessitates the identification of high-potential business ventures. This section offers a roadmap for pinpointing business opportunities poised for profitability, catering to both seasoned entrepreneurs and novices alike. These strategies are designed to unveil potential ventures that can catalyze your journey to financial success.

Skill and Passion Assessment: Begin by introspectively analyzing your talents, expertise, and passions. Identifying areas where you excel and are most enthusiastic about forms the bedrock for generating business ideas that resonate with your strengths and aspirations.

Market Trend Analysis: Keeping abreast of prevailing market trends and consumer demands is crucial. Spot growth-oriented industries and potential high-profit areas by identifying market voids that your business could fill, offering unique solutions or services.

Successful Business Model Study: Investigate and learn from thriving business models across various sectors. Understand their success drivers and contemplate how these principles could be adapted to your venture, fostering innovation and improvement.

In-depth Market Research: Conduct comprehensive research within your chosen industry to gauge target audience dynamics, competition, and market conditions. This deep dive aims to uncover nuanced insights into consumer needs and preferences, tailoring your offering to meet these demands effectively.

Idea Brainstorming and Validation: Engage in creative brainstorming to generate a plethora of business ideas. Critically assess each concept for its viability, scalability, and profitability potential. Validate your ideas through feedback from potential customers and industry experts, refining them based on this input.

Emerging Technology Exploration: Investigate how cutting-edge technologies might enhance or become integral to your business concept. Technologies such as AI, blockchain, or VR present novel opportunities for disruption across various industries.

Identifying lucrative business ideas is an art that balances one's skills, market demand, and personal passion. By adhering to these structured steps, you can uncover opportunities ripe for development, setting the stage for significant profit generation within a condensed timeframe.

Launching and Expanding a Prosperous Enterprise

Transforming the dream of becoming a millionaire in a year into reality is feasible with the right mindset, unwavering dedication, and a series of pragmatic steps. This section is crafted to guide individuals through the process of launching and scaling a thriving business from scratch, paving the way to achieve a seven-figure income within a year.

Identifying a profitable business niche is the first critical step. It requires aligning your venture with an area you're passionate about, coupled with market demand.

Conduct exhaustive market research to understand your intended audience deeply, pinpointing a unique value proposition that distinguishes your business.

Developing a comprehensive business plan is next, detailing your objectives, strategies, financial forecasts, and marketing approaches. This blueprint is instrumental in navigating the business's growth phases, ensuring focus and organization.

Establishing a compelling brand presence is crucial. This involves creating a professional logo, setting up an engaging website, and crafting content that resonates with your target demographic. Employ social media and digital marketing strategies to broaden your reach and attract potential customers.

To scale your business and enhance revenue streams, cultivating a robust professional network is indispensable. Engage with industry leaders, join professional bodies, and forge strategic partnerships to widen your market reach and access untapped customer segments.

A strong sales and customer service framework is also key to sustaining growth. Implement effective sales tactics and deliver unparalleled customer service to foster loyalty and secure repeat business.

Embracing continuous learning and self-improvement will keep you at the forefront of industry trends and innovation, vital for maintaining competitive edge and business growth.

In essence, embarking on and nurturing a successful business venture demands a blend of passion, strategy, and actionable steps. By meticulously following the outlined strategies, anyone can navigate the entrepreneurial landscape, overcoming challenges to realize their financial ambitions. Success in business is a cumulative result of persistent effort, strategic planning, and an enduring belief in one's capabilities.

Financial Leveraging E-Commerce for Advancement

In the digital era, e-commerce has emerged as a transformative force in the business world, offering entrepreneurs unprecedented opportunities to establish successful ventures from the ground up and engage with a global customer base. This section explores the essential steps required to harness e-commerce's potential, aiming to fast-track your progress towards earning a million dollars within a year from inception.

Understanding e-commerce's significance in the modern marketplace is fundamental. allows businesses to break geographical barriers, reaching a vast array of potential customers globally.

By building an online platform, you can present your products or services to an international audience around the clock, setting the stage for exponential growth and increased revenue.

Selecting a profitable niche is the inaugural step in your e-commerce journey. Conduct thorough market research to identify a unique segment with unmet needs that your online store can address, thereby carving out a distinct market position.

Setting up an e-commerce platform is the next pivotal step. Choose a suitable platform that aligns with your business model, utilizing customizable templates and user-friendly interfaces to build your online storefront. Optimize your site for mobile viewing to cater to the growing trend of mobile commerce.

Driving traffic to your e-commerce site is critical for business growth. Deploy targeted digital marketing strategies such as SEO, social media marketing, and paid advertising to attract potential customers. Collaborating with social media influencers can also amplify your reach and enhance brand visibility.

Exploring online marketplaces like Amazon, eBay, and Etsy can further augment your sales by tapping into their vast customer bases. This multi-channel approach can significantly boost your visibility and sales potential.

Providing exceptional customer service is paramount in building lasting customer relationships. Ensure a seamless purchasing experience, promptly address inquiries, and exceed customer expectations to foster loyalty and encourage repeat business.

In conclusion, leveraging e-commerce is a vital strategy in the quest to generate a million dollars within a year from zero. With dedication, strategic planning, and consistent effort, you can utilize the digital landscape to build a thriving online business, achieving financial success in record time.

1.Portfolio Diversification

2.Global Investment

3.Entrepreneurial Journey

4.Market Research

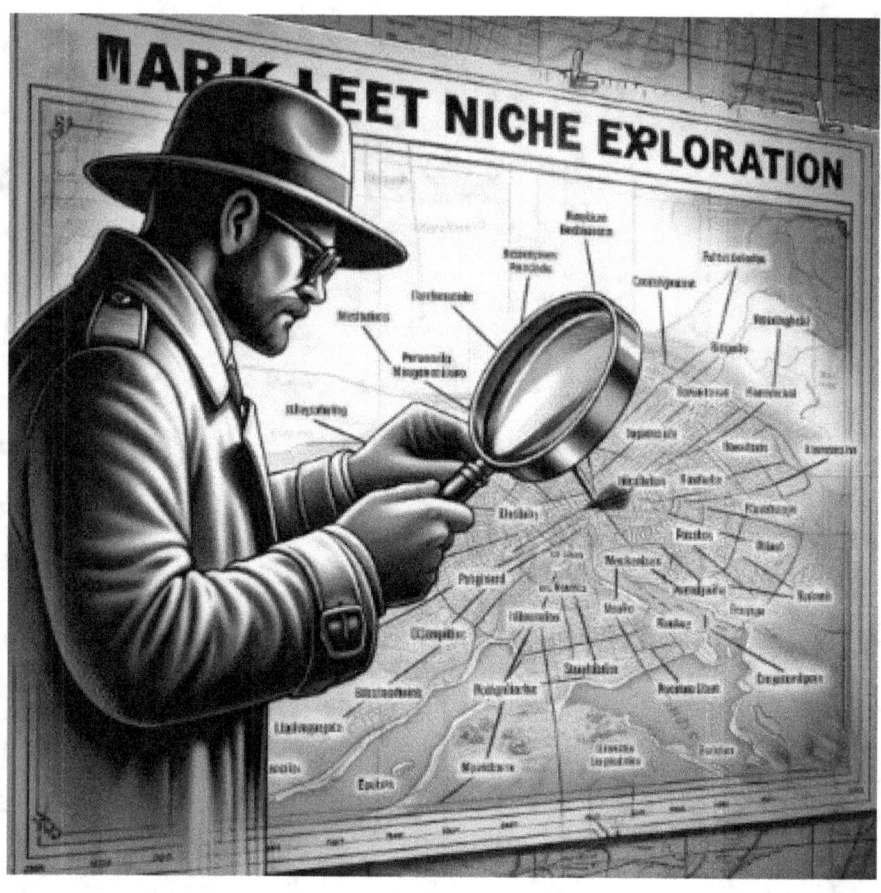

5.E-Commerce Platforma

6.Networking for Success

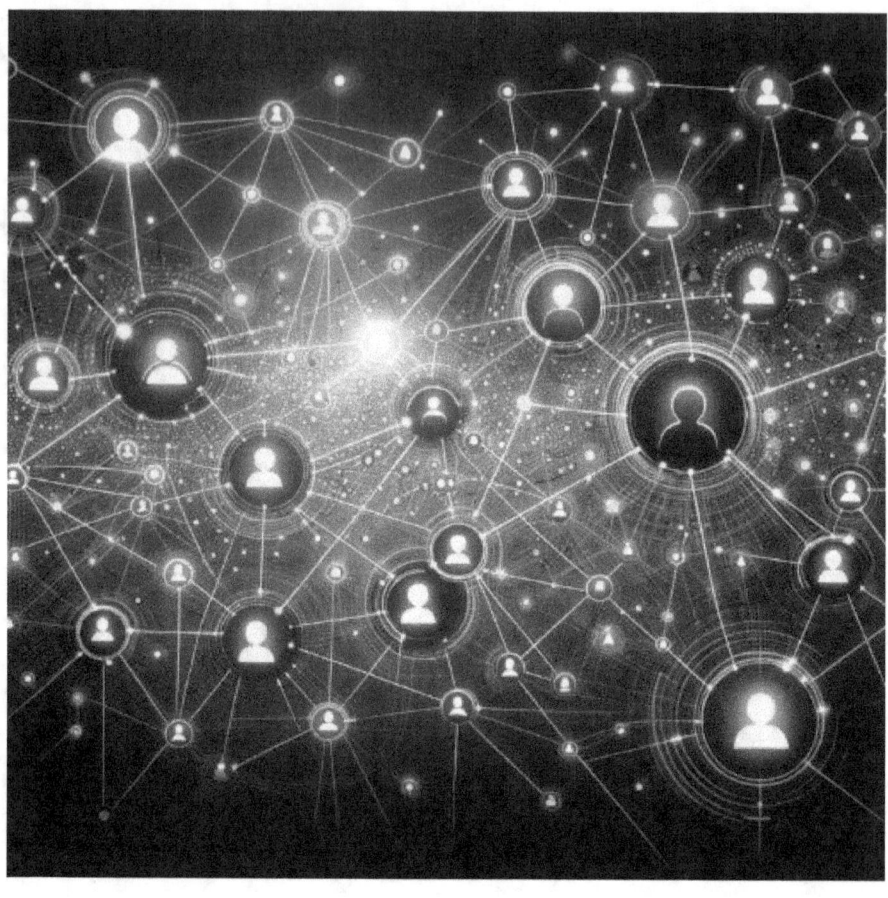

7.Social Media Marketing

8.Skill and Passion Assessment

9.Innovative Business Model

10.Customer Service Excellence

11.Strategic Partnership

Questionnaire: Strategic Diversification for Wealth Accumulation

Portfolio Diversification

- How well do you understand the concept of diversification in your investment portfolio?

- Are your investments spread across various asset classes such as equities, bonds, real estate, and more?

Global Investment

- Have you considered expanding your investment horizon to include international markets?
- Do you evaluate the geopolitical and economic stability of the regions you invest in?

Entrepreneurial Journey

- Have you assessed your skills and passions to identify potential business ventures?
- Are you actively engaging in market research to validate your business idea's potential?

Market Research

- How often do you analyze market trends to identify growth opportunities?
- Do you utilize market research to tailor your product or service offerings to meet consumer demands?

E-Commerce Platform

- Have you established an e-commerce platform for your business?
- Do you employ strategies to optimize your online platform for mobile users?

Networking for Success

- How actively do you network with industry leaders and potential collaborators?
- Do you participate in professional bodies or forums relevant to your business sector?

Social Media Marketing

- Are you leveraging social media platforms to enhance your business's visibility?
- Do you use targeted digital marketing strategies to drive traffic to your site?

Skill and Passion Assessment

- Have you conducted an introspective analysis to identify your core strengths for business success?
- Do you seek to align your business venture with your personal passions and expertise?

Innovative Business Model

- Are you exploring innovative business models to stand out in your industry?
- Do you study successful businesses to understand and implement their success strategies?

Customer Service Excellence

- Is exceptional customer service a cornerstone of your business strategy?
- Do you implement feedback mechanisms to continually improve customer service?

Strategic Partnership

- Have you considered forming strategic partnerships to expand your business reach?
- Do you assess the compatibility of potential partners with your business goals?

Scoring

Assign points to your answers based on the following:

- Yes (2 points): Indicates proactive engagement and a strategic approach.
- Somewhat (1 point): Shows some engagement, with room for improvement.
- No (0 points): Suggests a lack of engagement in this area.

Total Score Calculation

Sum of all responses: The total score reflects your strategic positioning for wealth accumulation through diversification, entrepreneurship, and e-commerce engagement.

Interpretation

- 33-44 points: You're effectively utilizing strategic diversification, entrepreneurial ventures, and e-commerce for wealth accumulation.
- 21-32 points: Moderate engagement in strategic areas, with significant room for growth and optimization.
- 0-20 points: Limited utilization of strategic diversification and entrepreneurial opportunities, indicating a need for a more proactive approach.

This scoring system helps identify areas of strength and those requiring more focus to optimize your strategies for wealth accumulation and reaching your financial goals.

Practical Steps that you could follow :

- Discovering High-Potential Business Ventures
- Skill and Passion Assessment:
- List your skills, expertise, and passions.
- Identify intersections where your skills meet a passion, indicating potential business ideas.

Market Trend Analysis:

- Regularly read industry reports, follow market news, and participate in relevant webinars or forums.
- Identify emerging trends and sectors with growth potential.

Successful Business Model Study:

- Analyze case studies of successful businesses.
- Note common factors contributing to their success and how these can apply to your idea.

In-depth Market Research:

- Conduct surveys, interviews, or use online tools to understand consumer needs and gaps in the current market.
- Validate your business idea with potential customers.

Idea Brainstorming and Validation:

- Organize brainstorming sessions, possibly using techniques like mind mapping.

- Validate ideas through prototypes or pilot services and gather feedback.

Emerging Technology Exploration:

- Stay informed about new technologies.
- Consider how these could be integrated into your business model for a competitive edge.
- Launching and Expanding a Prosperous Enterprise

Profitable Niche Identification:

- Align your business idea with personal passions and market demand.
- Use market research to refine your niche.

Comprehensive Business Plan Development:

- Outline your business strategy, financial projections, and marketing plans.
- Use this plan as a roadmap for your business journey.

Brand Presence Establishment:

- Design a memorable logo and user-friendly website.
- Utilize social media to build your brand and connect with your audience.

Professional Network Cultivation:

- Attend industry events and join professional organizations.
- Seek mentorship and collaboration opportunities.

Sales and Customer Service Framework:

- Develop effective sales strategies tailored to your audience.
- Prioritize exceptional customer service to build loyalty.
- Financial Leveraging E-Commerce for Advancement

E-Commerce Significance Understanding:

- Research the benefits and scope of e-commerce for your business.
- Identify how e-commerce can serve your business model.

Profitable Niche Selection for E-Commerce:

- Use market research to find an e-commerce niche with high demand and low competition.
- Validate the niche with potential customers.

E-Commerce Platform Setup:

- Choose an e-commerce platform that suits your business needs.
- Ensure your website is optimized for SEO and mobile users.

Traffic Driving Strategies:

- Implement SEO, social media marketing, and paid ads to attract visitors.
- Collaborate with influencers to extend your brand's reach.

Exceptional Customer Service Provision:

- Offer seamless purchasing experiences.

- Quickly address customer inquiries and feedback.

By following these steps, readers can systematically approach the identification of business opportunities, the launch and expansion of a business, and the strategic use of e-commerce to achieve financial goals. The journey to financial success requires dedication, continuous learning, and adapting to market changes

To effectively utilize the knowledge from the chapters on amplifying earnings potential, strategic investment, and diversification for wealth accumulation, I would suggest to follow these practical steps. This guide is trying to translate the concepts and strategies into actionable tasks that can help achieve the ambitious goal of generating significant financial growth within a year.

Amplifying Earnings Potential

Entrepreneurship Exploration:

- Brainstorm business ideas based on your interests, market needs, and potential for high returns.
- Conduct market research to validate your idea and identify your target audience.
- Develop a business plan outlining your strategy, financial projections, and marketing approach.

Investment in Skills:

- Identify skills in high demand within your industry or areas you're passionate about.

- Invest in courses, certifications, or workshops to enhance your expertise.

Digital Income Streams:

- Explore online platforms for freelancing, affiliate marketing, or creating and selling digital products.
- Build a personal brand on social media to attract opportunities and establish credibility.

Networking:

- Attend industry events, seminars, and workshops to connect with like-minded professionals.
- Join online forums and social media groups related to your field to exchange knowledge and find collaborations.
- Strategic Investment for Growth and Wealth Accumulation

Education on Investment:

- Dedicate time to learn about various investment vehicles (stocks, bonds, real estate, etc.).
- Use online resources, books, and courses to build your investment knowledge.

Market Research:

- Regularly follow financial news, market trends, and investment analyses.
- Utilize financial tools and platforms for in-depth research on potential investments.

Diversification Strategy:

- Allocate investments across different asset classes to spread risk.
- Consider long-term and short-term investments based on your financial goals.

Professional Advice:

- If possible, consult with a financial advisor to tailor your investment strategy to your personal risk tolerance and goals.
- Use robo-advisors for automated, algorithm-based investment recommendations.

Portfolio Review:

- Regularly assess your investment portfolio's performance.
- Rebalance your portfolio as needed to maintain alignment with your diversification strategy and financial objectives.
- Elevating Investment Portfolio Diversification

Asset Class Exploration:

- Research and identify various asset classes that align with your risk tolerance and financial goals.
- Diversify investments within each asset class (e.g., different sectors, industries, and geographies).

International Investments:

- Explore opportunities in emerging markets and international funds to add to your portfolio.

- Be aware of the risks and perform due diligence before investing in foreign markets.

Alternative Investments:

- Consider adding alternative investments like real estate, commodities, or digital currencies to your portfolio for further diversification.
- Understand the unique risks and opportunities each alternative investment presents.

Continuous Learning:

- Stay informed about global economic trends, market conditions, and new investment opportunities.
- Attend webinars, subscribe to investment newsletters, and follow thought leaders in the investment community.

Rebalancing Schedule:

- Set a regular schedule (e.g., quarterly, semi-annually) to review and rebalance your portfolio.
- Adjust your investment strategy based on performance, life changes, or shifts in financial goals.

Chapter 7: Harnessing the Dynamics of Professional Networking and Time Efficiency

Maximizing Opportunities Through Industry Conferences and Events

An integral component of the journey from aspiring individual to millionaire status is the strategic participation in industry conferences and events. Such platforms offer unparalleled opportunities for networking, knowledge acquisition, and keeping abreast of the latest trends and innovations within your sector. Catering to ambitious entrepreneurs, seasoned professionals, and those poised for a significant career transition, these gatherings are instrumental in propelling your financial aspirations toward the one-million-dollar mark within a year.

Networking forms the backbone of any successful entrepreneurial endeavor. Industry events provide an ideal setting for engaging with experts, potential investors, and accomplished entrepreneurs. These interactions facilitate the expansion of your professional network, unlocking access to invaluable resources. Forge new partnerships and collaborations, discover business opportunities, and edge closer to your financial objectives through these strategic connections.

Moreover, conferences serve as a conduit for gaining insights from sector leaders. Through keynote addresses, panel discussions, and workshops, attendees are privy to a wealth of knowledge that can revolutionize business strategies and decision-making processes. Learning from the successes and challenges of others enables you to navigate common pitfalls, leverage emerging trends, and maintain a competitive edge.

These events often spotlight pioneering products, services, and technological advancements pertinent to your niche. Experiencing these innovations firsthand equips you with the knowledge to adapt and evolve your business model accordingly. Staying attuned to the latest industry developments is vital for sustaining relevance and competitiveness, ensuring your journey from zero to millionaire remains on course.

To extract maximum value from industry events, meticulous preparation is essential. Familiarize yourself with the event agenda, pinpoint key speakers and exhibitors, and articulate clear objectives for your attendance. Seize networking opportunities by initiating conversations, exchanging business cards, and, most importantly, follow up on potential leads or connections post-event. Cultivating these relationships is pivotal in navigating the path to success.

Elevating Productivity through Time Management and Goal Prioritization

Embarking on the ambitious quest to generate a million dollars within a year underscores the necessity of prioritizing tasks and goals. In the absence of a focused plan, it's easy to succumb to distractions and lose sight of critical objectives. This section explores effective strategies for task prioritization, ensuring alignment with your overarching financial ambitions.

Commence with a reflective assessment of your core values, aspirations, and the rationale behind your million-dollar goal. This introspection clarifies your priorities, enabling you to tailor your actions accordingly. Following this, establish specific, measurable objectives. Segment your overarching target into attainable milestones, each accompanied by a defined timeline, fostering motivation and focus.

Assess the urgency and significance of each task using tools like Eisenhower's Urgent/Important Matrix. This method aids in categorizing tasks, allowing for strategic prioritization in alignment with your goals. Delegate or outsource peripheral activities to concentrate on core tasks that propel you toward financial success.

Periodic review and adaptation of your priorities are crucial as circumstances evolve. Remain receptive to feedback and continuously seek efficiencies in your approach to time and resource allocation.

Implementing practical time management techniques is paramount for maximizing productivity. Define clear, specific goals and prioritize tasks based on their contribution to your financial objectives. Develop a detailed schedule, adopt a disciplined approach to your daily routine, and eliminate time-wasting activities. Leverage technology and tools to streamline processes, and don't underestimate the importance of self-care in sustaining peak performance.

Overcoming procrastination is vital for maintaining momentum. Understand the root causes of procrastination, break down goals into manageable tasks, and create a structured plan with deadlines. Minimize distractions, seek accountability, and cultivate self-discipline to adhere to your plan. Celebrate incremental achievements to stay motivated.

In essence, mastering the art of networking at industry events and employing efficient time management and productivity strategies are crucial steps on the path to achieving a million dollars in a year. By embracing these practices, you can navigate the complexities of financial success, leveraging opportunities, and optimizing your efforts to turn your aspirations into reality.

1.Networking at Industry Conferences

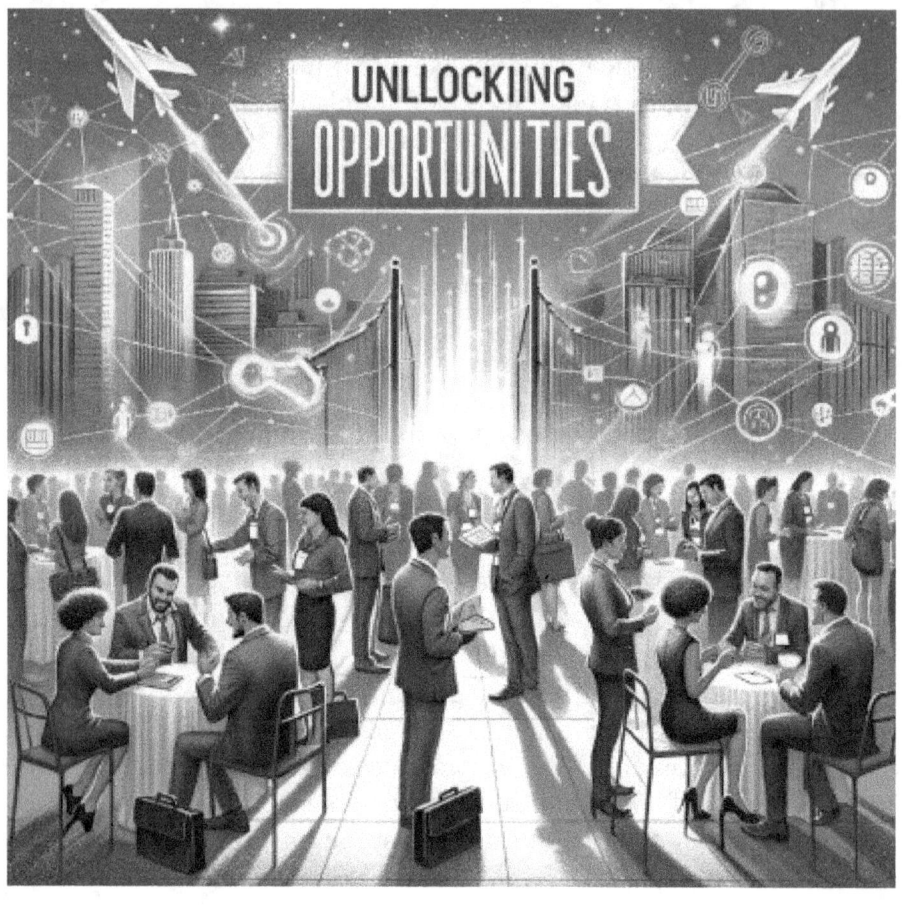

2.Learning from Industry Leaders

3.Global Industry Event

4.Strategic Networking

5.Prioritizing Tasks

6.Time Management

7.Goal Setting

8.Overcoming Procrastination

9.E-Commerce Success

10.Mastermind Group

Some suggestions of practical steps you can follow to achieve the knowleges from the above chapter "

Harnessing the Dynamics of Professional Networking and Time Efficiency

Attend Industry Conferences and Events:

- Research and identify key industry events relevant to your field.
- Set clear objectives for what you want to achieve from each event, such as meeting specific people or learning about new trends.

Effective Networking:

- Prepare a short pitch to introduce yourself and your business or professional interest.
- Focus on building genuine relationships rather than just collecting contacts. Follow up with new connections post-event.

Time Management and Goal Setting:

- Use tools like the Eisenhower Box to prioritize tasks based on urgency and importance.
- Set short-term and long-term goals, breaking them down into actionable steps with deadlines.

Overcoming Procrastination:

- Identify why you procrastinate (fear of failure, perfectionism, etc.) and address these underlying issues.
- Break tasks into smaller, manageable pieces and set a timer to work on tasks for short, focused periods.
- Cultivating a Mindset for Success

Identifying and Overcoming Limiting Beliefs:

- Write down your limiting beliefs and challenge them with evidence of your past successes or examples of others who have achieved similar goals.
- Replace negative thoughts with positive affirmations that reinforce your capability and potential.

Building Resilience:

- View setbacks as opportunities for growth. Reflect on what you can learn from each experience.
- Develop a support network of mentors, peers, and professionals who can provide advice and encouragement.

Fostering Positivity:

- Start each day by listing things you're grateful for to cultivate a positive mindset.
- Surround yourself with positive influences—people, books, podcasts—that inspire and motivate you.

Engaging in Self-Care:

- Incorporate activities into your routine that reduce stress and improve well-being, such as exercise, meditation, or hobbies.
- Recognize the signs of burnout and take steps to rest and recharge when needed.
- Practical Steps for Immediate Action

Create a Networking Strategy:

- Identify key individuals or groups within your industry you wish to connect with.
- Plan how to engage with these contacts, through social media, attending the same events, or direct outreach.

Optimize Your Daily Routine:

- Audit how you spend your time for one week to identify areas for improvement.
- Implement time-blocking techniques to dedicate specific hours to focused work, networking, learning, and personal time.

Set Measurable Goals:

- Define clear, measurable objectives for what you want to achieve in the next 12 months.
- Break these down into quarterly, monthly, and weekly goals, with specific actions for each.

Cultivate a Learning Mindset:

- Dedicate time each week to learning something new related to your industry or personal growth.
- Apply these learnings to your business or professional life to stay ahead of the curve.

Regular Reflection and Adjustment:

- Schedule regular check-ins with yourself to assess progress towards your goals.

- Be prepared to adjust your strategies based on what is or isn't working.

Chapter 8: Cultivating a Mindset for Success

Navigating Beyond Limiting Beliefs and Fears

A pivotal obstacle in the quest to amass one million dollars within a year is the challenge posed by our own limiting beliefs and fears. These internal barriers often emerge as formidable adversaries, hindering our progress towards financial aspirations. Recognizing and surmounting these hurdles is essential for unlocking our latent potential and charting a course towards success.

Limiting beliefs, those ingrained convictions that curtail our sense of possibility, often manifest as doubts about our competence, resources, or the feasibility of our financial objectives. Such thoughts, including beliefs like "I lack the necessary skills," or "Achieving such financial success in a year is unattainable," serve as self-imposed restrictions that shape our decisions and actions negatively.

To dismantle these limiting beliefs, the initial step involves their identification and confrontation. Reflect on the internal narratives that deter you from your financial pursuits. Challenge these beliefs by seeking evidence to the contrary, drawing inspiration from individuals who have realized similar ambitions or from your own experiences of overcoming adversity. Transitioning your mindset towards a focus on potential and opportunity allows for the replacement of limiting beliefs with empowering convictions.

Fears, including the dread of failure, rejection, or risk, often accompany our journey towards financial prosperity. It's imperative to recognize fear as a natural response but not allow it to dictate our actions. By breaking down your financial objectives into smaller, manageable tasks, you mitigate overwhelm and bolster confidence with each achieved milestone. Embrace calculated risks, viewing failures as integral learning moments rather than setbacks.

Cultivating a supportive network is invaluable for overcoming limiting beliefs and fears. Engage with mentors, coaches, or peers who share or support your financial goals. Their insights and encouragement can significantly bolster your confidence and belief in your capabilities.

Remember, transcending limiting beliefs and fears is a continual endeavor, necessitating persistent effort and introspection. As you navigate and conquer these internal obstacles, you unlock your true potential, facilitating a journey towards achieving a million dollars within a year.

Fostering Positivity and Resilience

Embarking on the ambitious journey to generate a million dollars within a year from the ground up necessitates the adoption of a positive and resilient mindset. Encountering obstacles and setbacks is inevitable; however, it is through a positive and resilient attitude that these challenges can be transformed into stepping stones towards your goal.

A positive outlook is crucial, enabling you to face every situation with optimism and assurance. It keeps your focus on the ultimate goal, even amidst difficulties, allowing you to perceive opportunities in the face of obstacles. Cultivating positivity enables efficient navigation towards success, transforming potential roadblocks into avenues of opportunity.

To nurture a positive mindset, immerse yourself in uplifting environments. Surround yourself with individuals who mirror your ambition and enthusiasm. Engage with mentors and participate in networks that reflect your aspirations, drawing inspiration from their success narratives. Their positive influence can invigorate your journey, instilling motivation and a sense of possibility.

Practicing gratitude reinforces a positive attitude. Daily reflections on aspects of your life for which you are thankful shift focus from challenges to the abundance present, laying a foundation for positivity to thrive.

Resilience, the capacity to recover from difficulties, complements positivity. Understand that setbacks are part and parcel of the success journey. Instead of succumbing to challenges, utilize them as learning experiences. Adopt failures as lessons that edify your path forward, enhancing your strategies and fortifying your resolve.

Self-care and compassion are pillars of resilience. Prioritize your well-being to maintain productivity and focus. Support from friends and family can provide emotional buoyancy, reminding you that setbacks are transient and do not define your worth or capabilities.

In summary, a positive and resilient mindset is instrumental for anyone venturing to make a million dollars in a year from scratch. By maintaining a positive outlook, embracing setbacks as lessons, and nurturing a supportive environment, you lay the groundwork for success on your path to financial achievement.

1.Enpowerment Through Evidence

2.Positive Mindset

3.Resilience in Adversity

4.Gratitude Practice

5.Networking for Growth

6.Breaking down Goals

7.Calculating Risk Taking

8. Mentorship and Support

9.Self-Care for Resilience

- Self-care for resilience -

10.Positivity in Challenge

Questionnaire: Cultivating a Mindset for Success

Navigating Beyond Limiting Beliefs and Fears

- Do you frequently encounter limiting beliefs that hinder your progress toward your financial goals?
- How often do you challenge your limiting beliefs with evidence of your capabilities or successes?
- Is fear of failure, rejection, or risk a significant barrier in your pursuit of financial prosperity?

- Do you break down your financial objectives into smaller, manageable tasks to mitigate overwhelm?
- How actively do you seek support from mentors, coaches, or peers to overcome your fears and limiting beliefs?

Fostering Positivity and Resilience

- How would you rate your ability to maintain a positive outlook, even in challenging situations?
- Do you surround yourself with individuals who reflect your ambition and enthusiasm for success?
- How frequently do you practice gratitude to reinforce a positive attitude towards your life and goals?
- How do you view setbacks or failures in your journey towards financial success?
- Do you prioritize self-care and seek support from friends and family to build resilience against challenges?

Scoring

Scoring for Each Question:

- Always (5 points): Indicates a strong, positive mindset and effective strategies to overcome challenges.
- Often (4 points): Shows a generally positive approach with occasional challenges.
- Sometimes (3 points): Reflects a moderate level of positivity and resilience, with room for improvement.
- Rarely (2 points): Suggests difficulties in maintaining a positive outlook and dealing with limiting beliefs.
- Never (1 point): Highlights significant areas for growth in developing a success-oriented mindset.

Total Score Calculation:

Add up the points from each question to get your total score.

Interpretation of Scores:

- **45-50 points:** You have a highly effective mindset for success, showing strong resilience and positivity.
- **35-44 points:** You're on the right path, with some areas to strengthen for better overcoming obstacles and fears.
- **25-34 points:** Moderate mindset effectiveness; focusing on positivity and tackling limiting beliefs could greatly aid your progress.
- **15-24 points:** Challenges in maintaining a positive outlook and resilience are apparent; targeted efforts can help improve your mindset.
- **10-14 points:** A significant need for development in cultivating a mindset for success; consider focusing on overcoming fears, fostering positivity, and building resilience.

This scoring helps you assess how well you're cultivating a mindset geared towards overcoming challenges and achieving financial success. Identifying areas for improvement can guide your efforts to develop a more resilient and positive approach to your financial goals.

Chapter 9: Architecting a Blueprint for Success

Transcending Limiting Beliefs and Overcoming Fears

A quintessential barrier on the path to financial achievement—amassing one million dollars within a single year—is the presence of limiting beliefs and ingrained fears. These psychological constraints can significantly impede progress, acting as invisible shackles that limit our potential. Recognizing and dismantling these barriers is vital for unlocking inherent capabilities and facilitating a trajectory towards success.

Limiting beliefs, those deep-seated convictions we hold about our own capabilities and potential, often manifest as doubts and negative self-talk. Phrases like "I lack the skills," "Success of this magnitude is unattainable," or "I'm not deserving of financial abundance" typify such beliefs. These narratives, however, are not reflections of reality but rather self-imposed constraints that dictate our actions and outcomes. Identifying and challenging these beliefs by seeking contrary evidence and drawing inspiration from success stories or personal victories is crucial. This process enables the substitution of disempowering beliefs with empowering ones, catalyzing a shift towards a mindset oriented around growth and possibility.

Fears, particularly those surrounding failure, rejection, and risk, can serve as significant deterrents. It's imperative to acknowledge fear as a natural reaction while refusing to let it govern decision-making. Decomposing overarching financial goals into smaller, actionable steps not only renders the endeavor less intimidating but also cultivates confidence through successive achievements. Embracing risk as a component of growth and perceiving failure as a conduit for learning and evolution is essential for progress.

Cultivating a supportive community—comprising mentors, coaches, and peers pursuing similar goals—can provide encouragement and diminish the impact of limiting beliefs and fears.

This network serves as a source of motivation, insight, and reassurance, reinforcing one's belief in their potential.

Overcoming limiting beliefs and fears is an iterative process, necessitating ongoing effort and introspection. As these internal barriers are navigated and surmounted, one's true potential is unleashed, paving the way towards achieving a significant financial milestone within a year.

Nurturing Positivity and Building Resilience

The ambition to generate a million dollars within a year, starting from scratch, demands not only strategic planning and execution but also the cultivation of a positive and resilient mindset. The journey is invariably marked by challenges and setbacks, making positivity and resilience indispensable allies in navigating the path to success.

A positive outlook enables the perception of obstacles as opportunities, fostering a solution-oriented approach to challenges. It facilitates sustained focus on the ultimate objective, even amidst adversity, allowing for the identification of creative solutions and pathways forward. Cultivating positivity involves surrounding oneself with sources of inspiration and motivation, including mentors, success stories, and a community of like-minded individuals. These influences imbue a sense of possibility and drive, essential for maintaining momentum.

Complementing positivity, resilience—the capacity to recover from setbacks and persist in the face of obstacles—is critical. It involves understanding that setbacks are integral to the success journey, serving not as deterrents but as stepping stones. Each challenge encountered and surmounted bolsters resilience, enhancing one's ability to navigate future hurdles more adeptly.

Practicing gratitude, acknowledging progress, and celebrating achievements, irrespective of scale, reinforce a positive and resilient mindset. These practices shift focus from the challenges at hand to the progress made and the learning acquired, laying a foundation for continued growth and persistence.

In essence, the cultivation of a positive and resilient attitude is paramount for anyone embarking on the ambitious quest to achieve significant financial success within a constrained timeframe. By adopting a mindset that embraces challenges as opportunities for growth and learning, the likelihood of realizing one's financial aspirations is markedly enhanced.

Embracing Failure as a Catalyst for Growth

Contrary to conventional perceptions, failure is not an end but a critical component of the success journey. It serves as an invaluable learning opportunity, providing insights that inform future strategies and decisions. Embracing failure as an integral part of the process is essential for anyone aspiring to transform their financial status significantly within a year.

Successful individuals across various domains have encountered and overcome failures, leveraging these experiences to refine their approaches and strategies. Viewing failure as a feedback mechanism rather than a setback enables a constructive response, facilitating adaptation and improvement.

The pursuit of a million dollars within a year, especially from a starting point of zero, inherently involves risks and the potential for failure. Recognizing failure as an opportunity for introspection and growth is key. Practical steps toward financial success necessitate a willingness to engage with failure positively, extracting lessons and applying these insights to future endeavors.

Moreover, failure cultivates resilience, enriching one's capacity to withstand and surmount future challenges. It fosters a mindset that views obstacles not as insurmountable barriers but as opportunities for learning and development.

In conclusion, embracing failure as a stepping stone rather than a stumbling block is crucial for navigating the path to financial success. It engenders a mindset of growth, resilience, and adaptability, essential qualities for anyone aspiring to achieve ambitious financial goals within a compressed timeframe.

1.Shattering Limiting Beliefs

2.Facing Fears

3.Network of Support

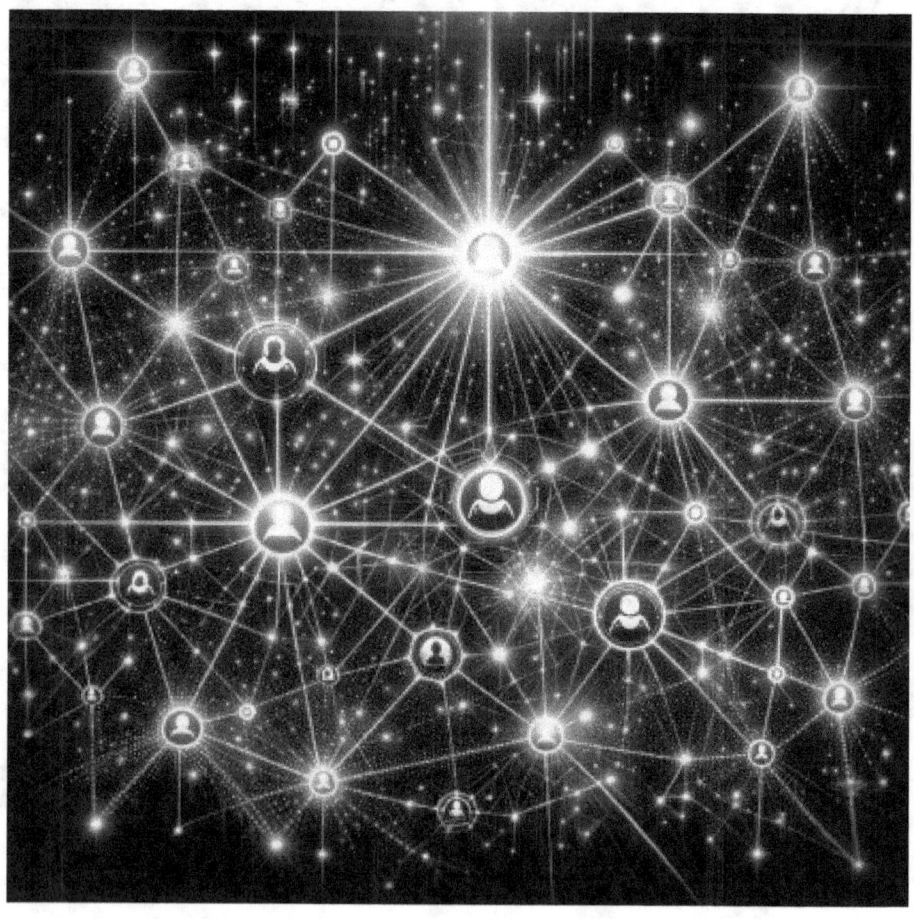

4.Growth from Failure

5.Cultivating Positivity

6.Building Resilience

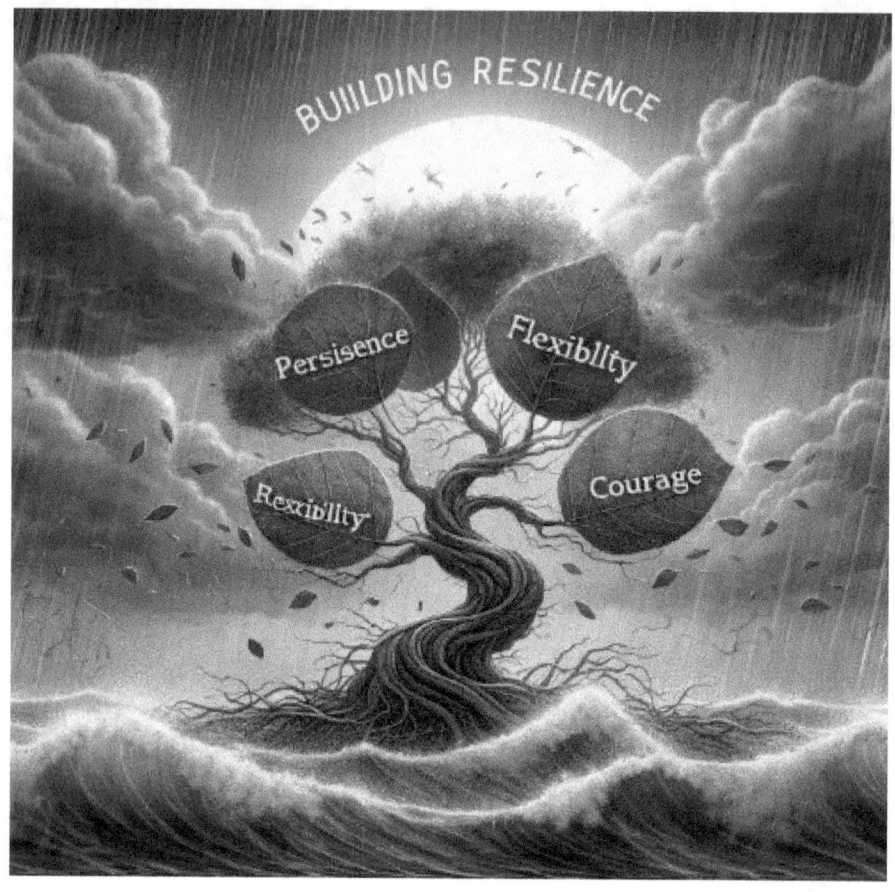

7.Path of Progress

8.Embracing Risk

9.Learning Cycle

Questionnaire: Architecting a Blueprint for Success

Transcending Limiting Beliefs and Overcoming Fears

Identification of Limiting Beliefs: Do you recognize specific limiting beliefs that hinder your financial progress?

Challenging Negative Self-Talk: How frequently do you counteract negative self-talk with evidence of your capabilities or achievements?

- Approach to Fear: Is fear of failure or risk a major obstacle in your pursuit of financial success?
- Actionable Steps for Goals: Do you break down your financial goals into smaller, manageable tasks?

Supportive Community Engagement: How actively do you engage with mentors, coaches, or peers to overcome fears and limiting beliefs?

- Nurturing Positivity and Building Resilience
- Maintaining a Positive Outlook: How would you rate your ability to stay positive in the face of financial challenges?
- Inspirational Environment: Do you surround yourself with sources of inspiration and motivation related to your financial goals?

Gratitude Practice: How often do you practice gratitude to reinforce positivity and resilience?

- View on Setbacks: Do you see setbacks as integral stepping stones rather than deterrents to success?
- Celebrating Achievements: How regularly do you acknowledge and celebrate your financial achievements, no matter the scale?
- Embracing Failure as a Catalyst for Growth

Perception of Failure: How do you perceive failure in the context of your financial goals?

- Learning from Failure: Are you able to extract and apply lessons from failures to improve future strategies?
- Risk Engagement: Do you view engaging with risks as a necessary part of achieving financial success?
- Failure as Feedback: How effectively do you use failure as a feedback mechanism for growth and improvement?

Building Resilience Through Failure: Do you believe that experiencing failure has strengthened your resilience and capacity to overcome future challenges?

Scoring

For Each Question:

- **Always (5 points):** Indicates a robust mindset well-equipped for overcoming obstacles and achieving financial success.
- **Often (4 points):** Shows a positive approach with some areas for further development.
- **Sometimes (3 points):** Reflects a moderate level of engagement with growth areas.
- **Rarely (2 points):** Suggests significant room for improvement in mindset and strategies.
- **Never (1 point):** Highlights critical areas needing immediate attention to foster success.

Total Score Calculation:

Sum the points for all responses.

Interpretation of Scores:

- **67-75 points:** You possess a strong, resilient mindset crucial for transcending limiting beliefs, embracing challenges, and achieving financial success.
- **51-66 points:** You're on a good path but need to enhance certain aspects of your mindset to effectively overcome fears and setbacks.
- **35-50 points:** Moderate mindset readiness; focus on nurturing positivity, resilience, and a constructive view of failure is needed.
- **15-34 points:** Limited engagement in success-fostering practices; significant work on overcoming limiting beliefs and embracing growth opportunities is essential.
- **Below 15 points:** Urgent need for mindset shift; consider seeking guidance to develop strategies for success, resilience, and positive thinking.

This scoring helps you assess the strength of your mindset and identify areas for growth in overcoming obstacles, nurturing a positive outlook, and leveraging failures for personal and financial growth.

Please find some suggestions of the steps you can take to try to take using the knowledges from this charter :

- Navigating Beyond Limiting Beliefs and Fears
- Identify Your Limiting Beliefs:
- Write down any beliefs that you think are holding you back from achieving your financial goals. Reflect on how these beliefs have affected your actions and decisions.

Challenge Your Limiting Beliefs:

- For each limiting belief, find evidence that contradicts it. This could be personal achievements that demonstrate your capabilities or examples of others who have succeeded in similar endeavors.

Break Down Financial Goals:

- Divide your overarching financial goal into smaller, achievable tasks. This makes the goal less overwhelming and helps build confidence as you achieve each task.

Seek Support:

- Actively engage with mentors, coaches, or peers who encourage your growth. Their insights and support can be invaluable in overcoming fears and limiting beliefs.
- Fostering Positivity and Resilience

Cultivate a Positive Outlook:

- Practice seeing challenges as opportunities. When faced with obstacles, ask yourself what you can learn and how you can grow from the experience.

Surround Yourself with Positivity:

- Spend time with people who inspire you and reflect the success you wish to achieve. Their positive influence can boost your motivation and outlook.

Practice Gratitude:

- Daily, list at least three things you're grateful for. This habit shifts your focus from what's lacking to the abundance already present in your life, fostering positivity.

View Setbacks as Stepping Stones:

- Instead of viewing setbacks as failures, see them as necessary steps towards your goal. Reflect on what each setback teaches you and how it can shape your path forward.
- Embracing Failure as a Catalyst for Growth

Reframe Your Perception of Failure:

- Change your view of failure from something to be avoided to a valuable learning experience. Recognize that each failure brings you closer to success by showing what doesn't work.

Extract Lessons from Failures:

- After a setback, take time to analyze what happened and why. Identify key takeaways and how you can apply this new knowledge to improve your future efforts.

Take Calculated Risks:

- Understand that risk is a part of achieving significant financial goals. Assess risks carefully, considering both potential downsides and upsides, and take steps to mitigate potential negative outcomes.

Use Failure as Feedback:

- See each failure as feedback on your journey, not a reflection of your worth or potential. Adjust your strategies and approaches based on what you learn from each experience.
- Practical Actions to Implement Today

Daily Reflection and Journaling:

- Spend a few minutes each day reflecting on your thoughts and feelings about your financial journey. Journaling can help you process your limiting beliefs and fears and recognize your growth over time.

Set Specific Weekly Goals:

- At the beginning of each week, set clear, achievable goals that align with your larger financial aspirations. Review and adjust these goals weekly to stay on track.

Engage in Continuous Learning:

- Dedicate time each week to learning something new related to your financial goals, whether through books, courses, or other resources. This commitment to growth can help overcome limiting beliefs and inspire new approaches.

Build a Support Network:

- Actively seek out and cultivate relationships with individuals who encourage and support your financial ambitions. This could involve joining relevant groups, attending workshops, or finding a mentor.

GOOD LUCK !

THE END !

APPENDIX "

For the good order sake , I am repeating the suggestions of the steps you can take to try to take using the knowledges from this book :

Step 1: Self-Assessment and Mindset Adjustment

Reflect on your current mindset regarding wealth and success. Recognize any limiting beliefs and commit to adopting a growth and success-oriented mindset.

Complete the questionnaire provided in the text to assess your current mindset and readiness for financial success. This will help identify areas for improvement.

Step 2: Goal Setting and Visualization

- Define clear, specific financial goals for the short term (1 year) and long term (5 years and beyond).

Make them SMART: Specific, Measurable, Achievable, Relevant, and Time-bound.

- Create a vision board or write a detailed description of your life once you achieve these financial goals. Regularly visualize your success to maintain motivation.

Step 3: Financial Analysis and Planning

- Conduct a thorough review of your current financial situation, including income, expenses, assets, and liabilities.
- Identify areas for cost reduction and increase in income. This might involve budget adjustments, lifestyle changes, and exploring additional income streams.
- Develop a detailed financial plan that outlines steps to achieve your goals, including savings targets, investment strategies, and debt reduction plans.

Step 4: Implementation and Discipline

- Implement your financial plan with discipline. Use tools like budget trackers, financial planning apps, or spreadsheets to monitor your progress.
- Adjust your plan as necessary, based on changes in your financial situation or goals.

Step 5: Education and Growth

- Commit to continuous learning about personal finance, investment, and wealth management. Read books, attend workshops, or take courses to enhance your knowledge and skills.
- Network with successful individuals who have achieved similar financial goals. Learn from their experiences and apply relevant advice to your situation.

Step 6: Resilience and Persistence

- Prepare for setbacks and challenges. Develop resilience by viewing failures as learning opportunities.
- Stay persistent in your efforts. Remember that achieving significant financial success often takes time and continuous effort.

Step 7: Evaluation and Adjustment

- Regularly evaluate your financial progress against your goals. Use the scoring guide provided in the text to assess your mindset and strategy effectiveness.
- Make necessary adjustments to your financial plan and strategies based on your evaluation.

Step 8: Reflection and Mindset Reinforcement

- Reflect on your journey periodically. Acknowledge your achievements and areas of improvement.
- Reinforce a positive and success-oriented mindset. Celebrate successes, no matter how small, to maintain motivation and commitment to your financial goals.

Step 9: Sharing and Mentoring

- Once you've made significant progress or achieved your goals, consider sharing your knowledge and experiences with others. Mentoring or guiding others can reinforce your own understanding and commitment to financial success.

Step 10: Scaling and Diversification

- Explore opportunities for scaling your income and diversifying your investment portfolio. Consider more advanced financial strategies to protect and grow your wealth further.

Discovering High-Potential Business Ventures

Skill and Passion Assessment:

List your skills, expertise, and passions.

- Identify intersections where your skills meet a passion, indicating potential business ideas.

Market Trend Analysis:

- Regularly read industry reports, follow market news, and participate in relevant webinars or forums.
- Identify emerging trends and sectors with growth potential.

Successful Business Model Study:

- Analyze case studies of successful businesses.
- Note common factors contributing to their success and how these can apply to your idea.

In-depth Market Research:

- Conduct surveys, interviews, or use online tools to understand consumer needs and gaps in the current market.
- Validate your business idea with potential customers.

Idea Brainstorming and Validation:

- Organize brainstorming sessions, possibly using techniques like mind mapping.
- Validate ideas through prototypes or pilot services and gather feedback.

Emerging Technology Exploration:

- Stay informed about new technologies.
- Consider how these could be integrated into your business model for a competitive edge.
- Launching and Expanding a Prosperous Enterprise

Profitable Niche Identification:

- Align your business idea with personal passions and market demand.
- Use market research to refine your niche.
- Comprehensive Business Plan Development:
- Outline your business strategy, financial projections, and marketing plans.
- Use this plan as a roadmap for your business journey.

Brand Presence Establishment:

- Design a memorable logo and user-friendly website.
- Utilize social media to build your brand and connect with your audience.
- Professional Network Cultivation:
- Attend industry events and join professional organizations.
- Seek mentorship and collaboration opportunities.

Sales and Customer Service Framework:

- Develop effective sales strategies tailored to your audience.

- Prioritize exceptional customer service to build loyalty.
- Financial Leveraging E-Commerce for Advancement

E-Commerce Significance Understanding:

- Research the benefits and scope of e-commerce for your business.
- Identify how e-commerce can serve your business model.

Profitable Niche Selection for E-Commerce:

- Use market research to find an e-commerce niche with high demand and low competition.
- Validate the niche with potential customers.

E-Commerce Platform Setup:

- Choose an e-commerce platform that suits your business needs.
- Ensure your website is optimized for SEO and mobile users.

Traffic Driving Strategies:

- Implement SEO, social media marketing, and paid ads to attract visitors.
- Collaborate with influencers to extend your brand's reach.

Exceptional Customer Service Provision:

- Offer seamless purchasing experiences.
- Quickly address customer inquiries and feedback.

By following these steps, readers can systematically approach the identification of business opportunities, the launch and expansion of a business, and the strategic use of e-commerce to achieve financial goals. The journey to financial success requires dedication, continuous learning, and adapting to market changes

To effectively utilize the knowledge from the chapters on amplifying earnings potential, strategic investment, and diversification for wealth accumulation, I would suggest to follow these practical steps. This guide is trying to translate the concepts and strategies into actionable tasks that can help achieve the ambitious goal of generating significant financial growth within a year.

Amplifying Earnings Potential

Entrepreneurship Exploration:

- Brainstorm business ideas based on your interests, market needs, and potential for high returns.
- Conduct market research to validate your idea and identify your target audience.
- Develop a business plan outlining your strategy, financial projections, and marketing approach.

Investment in Skills:

- Identify skills in high demand within your industry or areas you're passionate about.
- Invest in courses, certifications, or workshops to enhance your expertise.

Digital Income Streams:

- Explore online platforms for freelancing, affiliate marketing, or creating and selling digital products.
- Build a personal brand on social media to attract opportunities and establish credibility.

Networking:

- Attend industry events, seminars, and workshops to connect with like-minded professionals.
- Join online forums and social media groups related to your field to exchange knowledge and find collaborations.
- Strategic Investment for Growth and Wealth Accumulation

Education on Investment:

- Dedicate time to learn about various investment vehicles (stocks, bonds, real estate, etc.).
- Use online resources, books, and courses to build your investment knowledge.

Market Research:

- Regularly follow financial news, market trends, and investment analyses.
- Utilize financial tools and platforms for in-depth research on potential investments.

Diversification Strategy:

- Allocate investments across different asset classes to spread risk.

- Consider long-term and short-term investments based on your financial goals.

Professional Advice:

- If possible, consult with a financial advisor to tailor your investment strategy to your personal risk tolerance and goals.
- Use robo-advisors for automated, algorithm-based investment recommendations.

Portfolio Review:

- Regularly assess your investment portfolio's performance.
- Rebalance your portfolio as needed to maintain alignment with your diversification strategy and financial objectives.
- Elevating Investment Portfolio Diversification

Asset Class Exploration:

- Research and identify various asset classes that align with your risk tolerance and financial goals.
- Diversify investments within each asset class (e.g., different sectors, industries, and geographies).

International Investments:

- Explore opportunities in emerging markets and international funds to add to your portfolio.
- Be aware of the risks and perform due diligence before investing in foreign markets.

Alternative Investments:

- Consider adding alternative investments like real estate, commodities, or digital currencies to your portfolio for further diversification.
- Understand the unique risks and opportunities each alternative investment presents.

Continuous Learning:

- Stay informed about global economic trends, market conditions, and new investment opportunities.
- Attend webinars, subscribe to investment newsletters, and follow thought leaders in the investment community.

Rebalancing Schedule:

- Set a regular schedule (e.g., quarterly, semi-annually) to review and rebalance your portfolio.
- Adjust your investment strategy based on performance, life changes, or shifts in financial goals.
- Harnessing the Dynamics of Professional Networking and Time Efficiency

Attend Industry Conferences and Events:

- Research and identify key industry events relevant to your field.
- Set clear objectives for what you want to achieve from each event, such as meeting specific people or learning about new trends.

Effective Networking:

- Prepare a short pitch to introduce yourself and your business or professional interest.
- Focus on building genuine relationships rather than just collecting contacts. Follow up with new connections post-event.

Time Management and Goal Setting:

- Use tools like the Eisenhower Box to prioritize tasks based on urgency and importance.
- Set short-term and long-term goals, breaking them down into actionable steps with deadlines.

Overcoming Procrastination:

- Identify why you procrastinate (fear of failure, perfectionism, etc.) and address these underlying issues.
- Break tasks into smaller, manageable pieces and set a timer to work on tasks for short, focused periods.
- Cultivating a Mindset for Success

Identifying and Overcoming Limiting Beliefs:

- Write down your limiting beliefs and challenge them with evidence of your past successes or examples of others who have achieved similar goals.
- Replace negative thoughts with positive affirmations that reinforce your capability and potential.

Building Resilience:

- View setbacks as opportunities for growth. Reflect on what you can learn from each experience.
- Develop a support network of mentors, peers, and professionals who can provide advice and encouragement.

Fostering Positivity:

- Start each day by listing things you're grateful for to cultivate a positive mindset.
- Surround yourself with positive influences—people, books, podcasts—that inspire and motivate you.

Engaging in Self-Care:

- Incorporate activities into your routine that reduce stress and improve well-being, such as exercise, meditation, or hobbies.
- Recognize the signs of burnout and take steps to rest and recharge when needed.
- Practical Steps for Immediate Action

Create a Networking Strategy:

- Identify key individuals or groups within your industry you wish to connect with.
- Plan how to engage with these contacts, through social media, attending the same events, or direct outreach.

Optimize Your Daily Routine:

- Audit how you spend your time for one week to identify areas for improvement.

- Implement time-blocking techniques to dedicate specific hours to focused work, networking, learning, and personal time.

Set Measurable Goals:

- Define clear, measurable objectives for what you want to achieve in the next 12 months.
- Break these down into quarterly, monthly, and weekly goals, with specific actions for each.

Cultivate a Learning Mindset:

- Dedicate time each week to learning something new related to your industry or personal growth.
- Apply these learnings to your business or professional life to stay ahead of the curve.

Regular Reflection and Adjustment:

- Schedule regular check-ins with yourself to assess progress towards your goals.
- Be prepared to adjust your strategies based on what is or isn't working.
- Navigating Beyond Limiting Beliefs and Fears

Identify Your Limiting Beliefs:

- Write down any beliefs that you think are holding you back from achieving your financial goals. Reflect on how these beliefs have affected your actions and decisions.

Challenge Your Limiting Beliefs:

- For each limiting belief, find evidence that contradicts it. This could be personal achievements that demonstrate your capabilities or examples of others who have succeeded in similar endeavors.

Break Down Financial Goals:

- Divide your overarching financial goal into smaller, achievable tasks. This makes the goal less overwhelming and helps build confidence as you achieve each task.

Seek Support:

- Actively engage with mentors, coaches, or peers who encourage your growth. Their insights and support can be invaluable in overcoming fears and limiting beliefs.
- Fostering Positivity and Resilience

Cultivate a Positive Outlook:

- Practice seeing challenges as opportunities. When faced with obstacles, ask yourself what you can learn and how you can grow from the experience.

Surround Yourself with Positivity:

- Spend time with people who inspire you and reflect the success you wish to achieve. Their positive influence can boost your motivation and outlook.

Practice Gratitude:

- Daily, list at least three things you're grateful for. This habit shifts your focus from what's lacking to the abundance already present in your life, fostering positivity.

View Setbacks as Stepping Stones:

- Instead of viewing setbacks as failures, see them as necessary steps towards your goal. Reflect on what each setback teaches you and how it can shape your path forward.
- Embracing Failure as a Catalyst for Growth

Reframe Your Perception of Failure:

- Change your view of failure from something to be avoided to a valuable learning experience. Recognize that each failure brings you closer to success by showing what doesn't work.

Extract Lessons from Failures:

- After a setback, take time to analyze what happened and why. Identify key takeaways and how you can apply this new knowledge to improve your future efforts.

Take Calculated Risks:

- Understand that risk is a part of achieving significant financial goals. Assess risks carefully, considering both potential downsides and upsides, and take steps to mitigate potential negative outcomes.

Use Failure as Feedback:

- See each failure as feedback on your journey, not a reflection of your worth or potential. Adjust your strategies and approaches based on what you learn from each experience.
- Practical Actions to Implement Today

Daily Reflection and Journaling:

- Spend a few minutes each day reflecting on your thoughts and feelings about your financial journey. Journaling can help you process your limiting beliefs and fears and recognize your growth over time.

Set Specific Weekly Goals:

- At the beginning of each week, set clear, achievable goals that align with your larger financial aspirations. Review and adjust these goals weekly to stay on track.

Engage in Continuous Learning:

- Dedicate time each week to learning something new related to your financial goals, whether through books, courses, or other resources. This commitment to growth can help overcome limiting beliefs and inspire new approaches.

Build a Support Network:

- Actively seek out and cultivate relationships with individuals who encourage and support your financial ambitions. This could involve joining relevant groups, attending workshops, or finding a mentor.

Disclaimer

The information provided in this book, including but not limited to text, graphics, images, diagrams, and other material, is for informational purposes only and is not intended to replace or substitute for any professional,financial, medical, legal, or other advice. The content of this book represents the author's personal views and experiences and is presented for educational and informational purposes only. The author and publisher make no representations or warranties of any kind, express or implied, about the completeness, accuracy, reliability, suitability, or availability with respect to the book or the information, products, services, or related graphics contained in the book for any purpose.

Any reliance you place on such information is therefore strictly at your own risk. In no event will the author or publisher be liable for any loss or damage including without limitation, indirect or consequential loss or damage, or any loss or damage whatsoever arising from loss of data or profits arising out of,or in connection with, the use of this book. While attempts have been made to verify the accuracy of the information provided in this publication, neither the author nor the publisher assumes any responsibility for errors, omissions, or contrary interpretations of the

subject matter herein. This book may contain references to other books,products, or services that are not controlled by or affiliated with the author or publisher. Such references do not imply the endorsement or approval of such books, products, or services.

This disclaimer is not intended to limit or exclude any liability that cannot be legally limited or excluded, including but not limited to death or personal injury caused by negligence. Readers are cautioned to consult with professional advisors for advice specific to their circumstances. The health-related information provided in the book is not intended to be a substitute for professional medical advice, diagnosis, or treatment. Always

seek the advice of your physician or other qualified health providers with any questions you may have regarding a medical condition or health objectives. The technical and scientific information presented is based on the author's personal understanding and experiences and should not be considered

exhaustive or up-to-date. Readers are encouraged to conduct their own research and consult with professionals in the respective fields for the most current information.

By using this book, you agree that the exclusions and limitations of liability set out in this disclaimer are reasonable. If you do not think they are reasonable, you must not use this book.

www.ingramcontent.com/pod-product-compliance
Lightning Source LLC
Chambersburg PA
CBHW071042290526
45795CB00004B/1276